American Revolution 1775–83

Patriot
VERSUS
Loyalist

Si Sheppard

Illustrated by A.

OSPREY PUBLISHING
Bloomsbury Publishing Plc
Kemp House, Chawley Park, Cumnor Hill, Oxford OX2 9PH, UK
29 Earlsfort Terrace, Dublin 2, Ireland
1385 Broadway, 5th Floor, New York, NY 10018, USA
E-mail: info@ospreypublishing.com
www.ospreypublishing.com

OSPREY is a trademark of Osprey Publishing Ltd

First published in Great Britain in 2022

A catalog record for this book is available from the British Library.

ISBN: PB 9781472844200; eBook 9781472844217;
ePDF 9781472844187; XML 9781472844194

22 23 24 25 26   10 9 8 7 6 5 4 3 2 1

Maps by www.bounford.com
Index by Rob Munro
Typeset by PDQ Digital Media Solutions, Bungay, UK
Printed and bound in India by Replika Press Private Ltd.

MIX
Paper from
responsible sources
FSC® C016779

Osprey Publishing supports the Woodland Trust, the UK's leading
woodland conservation charity.

To find out more about our authors and books visit
www.ospreypublishing.com. Here you will find extracts, author
interviews, details of forthcoming events and the option to sign up for
our newsletter.

Dedicated to Westchester County: History, Heritage, & Home.

Artist's note

Readers may care to note that the original paintings from which the
color plates in this book were prepared are available for private sale. All
reproduction copyright whatsoever is retained by the publishers. All
inquiries should be addressed to:

scorpiopaintings@btinternet.com

The publishers regret that they can enter into no correspondence upon
this matter.

CONTENTS

Introduction

War takes two forms: interstate (between countries) and intrastate (within a country). Since 1945, it is the latter form that has predominated globally, from Yugoslavia to Rwanda. This has not in any way de-escalated the lethality of armed conflict, however. In fact, the collapse of the domestic social order that creates, pervades, and persists long after the formal conclusion to such a struggle can leave far deeper scars. The experience of defeat, even occupation, at the conclusion of a formal war against a rival state can bring a society together – at the very least, an occupying foreign army will eventually go home – but those who have endured the horrors of domestic strife must live with the perpetrators of such violence as a permanent presence in their lives as neighbors, even members of the same family.

One observer with firsthand experience of traveling through a zone of civil war noted his detailed impressions of the psychological toll such intramural violence takes on members of the communities affected. "To every question they gave such an answer as would please the inquirer; or, if they despaired of pleasing, such a one as would not provoke him," he recorded of the individuals he interacted with:

> Fear was, apparently, the only passion by which they were animated. The power of volition seemed to have deserted them. They were not civil, but obsequious; not obliging, but subservient. They yielded with a kind of apathy, and very quietly, what you asked, and what they supposed it impossible for them to retain ... Both their countenances and the motions had lost every trace of animation and of feeling. The features were smoothed, not into serenity, but apathy; and, instead of being settled in the attitude of quiet thinking, strongly indicated that all thought beyond what was merely instinctive, had fled their minds forever. (Dwight 1822: 491)

This account reads like testimony provided by a nongovernmental organization reporting from such contemporary crisis states as Syria or Yemen. In fact, it is an

A Loyalist is tarred and feathered before being hanged by Patriots – a not uncommon sight during the American Revolutionary War. Those refusing to transfer their allegiance from Crown to Congress could pay a heavy price for their recalcitrance. One Loyalist from Rhinebeck in Dutchess County, New York, was beaten, robbed, and then tarred and feathered by a mob for not signing the Continental Association. The same day another mob tarred him again and, for good measure, tarred and feathered his horse too. (Hulton Archive/ Getty Images)

entry from the journal of a chaplain, Dr. Timothy Dwight, who was stationed with Patriot forces in Westchester County, New York, in the fall of 1777.

The American Revolutionary War (1775–83) was a war of colonial secession from the imperial construct of British power, but also the justification for, and a theater of operations in, a world war, one in a succession of such conflicts between 1688 and 1815. For most of those caught up in this struggle, the primary experience was of civil war; of communities, even families, sundered, of neighbor turning against neighbor. The standing armies of the two sides might have occupied any given territory at any time, according to the dictates of strategic imperative. In so doing, they exacerbated tensions within that territory, inflaming latent loyalties to Crown or Congress into overt hostilities; and in the wake of a formal campaign, once the regular armies of one or other side had departed, those hostilities continued to play out in the ever-escalating brutality of raid and counterraid, atrocity and reprisal, that shocked witnesses of all ranks. From out of this maelstrom emerged the United States of America.

While the American Revolutionary War is commemorated for its great set-piece battles and sieges, just as decisive to the outcome were the small-unit actions undertaken by individuals operating on their own recognizance, motivated by personal imperatives, little recognized at the time and even less so now beyond rusting street signs and fading gravestones. These are their stories.

MAP KEY

1 **April 19, 1775:** Lexington and Concord, MA. Patriot Minutemen fire the first shots of a world war.

2 **December 9, 1775:** Great Bridge, VA. Loyalist defeat solidifies Patriot control of Virginia.

3 **December 22, 1775:** Great Cane Brake, SC. Patriots defeat Loyalists seeking to ally with the Cherokee.

4 **February 27, 1776:** Moore's Creek Bridge, NC. Patriots defeat transplanted Scottish Highlander Loyalists.

5 **August 6, 1777:** Oriskany, NY. Loyalists and First Nations allies under Lieutenant Colonel Sir John Johnson and Joseph Brant (Thayendanegea) ambush and defeat Patriots.

6 **July 3, 1778:** Wyoming Valley, PA. Loyalists and First Nations allies under Lieutenant Colonel John Butler defeat Patriots and despoil their communities.

7 **September 17, 1778:** German Flatts, NY. Loyalists and First Nations allies under Captain William Caldwell and Brant ransack Patriot communities.

8 **November 11, 1778:** Cherry Valley, NY. Loyalists and First Nations allies under Captain Walter Butler and Brant ransack Patriot communities.

9 **February 14, 1779:** Kettle Creek, GA. Patriots under Colonel Andrew Pickens defeat a Loyalist force twice their number.

10 **July 22, 1779:** Minisink, NY. First Nations warriors and Loyalists under Brant defeat Patriots.

11 **July 12, 1780:** Huck's Defeat, SC. Patriots under Colonel William Bratton defeat Loyalists under Captain Christian Huck.

12 **July 26, 1780:** Thicketty Fort, SC. Patriots under Colonel Isaac Shelby force the Loyalist garrison to surrender.

13 **August 6, 1780:** Hanging Rock, SC. Patriots under Brigadier General Thomas Sumter storm the Loyalist fort.

14 **August 18, 1780:** Fishing Creek, SC. Loyalists under Lieutenant-Colonel Banastre Tarleton surprise and rout Patriots under Sumter.

15 **August 19, 1780:** Musgrove Mill, SC. Militia Colonel Elijah Clarke and Shelby defeat Loyalists.

16 **September 30, 1780:** Black Mingo Creek, SC. Following up on his first victories at Britton's Neck and Blue Savannah on September 4, Lieutenant Colonel Francis Marion defeats Loyalists.

17 **October 7, 1780:** Kings Mountain, SC. Patriots annihilate Loyalists under Major Patrick Ferguson, collapsing the left flank of British forces under Lieutenant-General Charles, Lord Cornwallis and spiking his invasion of North Carolina.

18 **October 19, 1780:** Stone Arabia, NY. Loyalists and First Nations allies under Johnson and Brant defeat a Patriot force under Colonel John Brown, who is killed. Later that day, Johnson and Brant are repulsed by Patriot forces under Brigadier General Robert Van Rensselaer at Klock's Field, but withdraw having devastated the Mohawk Valley.

19 **November 20, 1780:** Blackstock's Farm, SC. Sumter gains his revenge by defeating Tarleton.

20 **January 5, 1781:** Richmond, VA. Governor Thomas Jefferson flees the state capital as Loyalists under Brigadier General Benedict Arnold sack the town.

21 **March 6, 1781:** Lynches Creek, SC. Sumter is defeated by Loyalists under Major Thomas Fraser.

22 **June 4, 1781:** Monticello, VA. Jefferson flees his plantation just ahead of a raid by Tarleton, who seizes Charlottesville, the temporary state capital of Virginia.

23 **June 5, 1781:** Augusta, GA. Patriots under Clarke force the surrender of the Loyalist garrison under Lieutenant Colonel Thomas Brown.

24 **August 24, 1781:** Lochry's Defeat, IN. First Nations warriors under Brant ambush and wipe out a Patriot force under Colonel Archibald Lochry.

25 **August 30, 1781:** Parker's Ferry, SC. Brigadier General Francis Marion defeats Loyalists under Major Thomas Fraser.

26 **September 13, 1781:** Lindley's Mill, NC. Loyalists under Colonel David Fanning returning from a raid on Hillsborough, the state capital of North Carolina, are ambushed by Patriots but push their way through to Wilmington.

27 **June 4–6, 1782:** Sandusky River, OH. A coalition of First Nations warriors repulses an invasion by Patriot Colonel William Crawford, who is captured and subsequently tortured to death.

28 **August 19, 1782:** Blue Licks, KY. First Nations warriors and Loyalists under Caldwell ambush and defeat Patriots, among them Daniel Boone, whose son, Israel, is killed.

29 **August 29, 1782:** Wadboo Plantation, SC. Marion defeats Loyalists under Fraser.

30 **November 10, 1782:** Chillicothe, OH. Patriot Brigadier General George Rogers Clark leads a militia force to victory over the Shawnee in the last major battle of the war.

Gulf of
St. Lawrence

Cape
Breton I.

Louisbourg

ST. JOHN'S
ISLAND

Charlottetown

NOVA
SCOTIA

Halifax

Annapolis
Royal

St. John

MAINE
(IN MASSACHUSETTS)

NEW HAMPSHIRE

Falmouth

Portsmouth

MASSACHUSETTS

Boston

RHODE ISLAND

Providence

CONNECTICUT

NEW YORK

ATLANTIC OCEAN

Quebec

Montreal

PROVINCE
OF QUEBEC

ONEIDA

MOHAWK

ONONDAGA

CAYUGA

TUSCARORA

SENECA

Albany

New
Haven

New York

Trenton

NEW JERSEY

Philadelphia

PENNSYLVANIA

Wilmington

DELAWARE

MARYLAND

Baltimore

Annapolis

Alexandria

Richmond

VIRGINIA

Charlottesville

Williamsburg

Yorktown

NORTH CAROLINA

Hillsborough

New Bern

Wilmington

SOUTH CAROLINA

Charlotte

Charleston

Savannah

GEORGIA

Ninety Six

Augusta

EAST
FLORIDA

St. Augustine

CHEROKEE

CREEK

WEST
FLORIDA

Pensacola

Gulf of Mexico

CHOCTAW

Fort Panmure

Baton Rouge

New Orleans

LOUISIANA
(SPAIN)

St. Louis

Kaskaskia

Mississippi

Missouri

Arkansas

Tennessee

Ohio

Vincennes

SHAWNEE

MIAMI

INDIAN RESERVE

DELAWARE

Detroit

Fort Niagara

Lake Ontario

Lake Erie

Lake Huron

Lake Michigan

Lake
Superior

Sault Ste. Marie

RUPERT'S
LAND

Ottawa

St. Lawrence

Legend:

Thirteen Colonies

The Indian Reserve

Crown Territory

The Proclamation Line of 1763

Thirteen Colonies settlements

Other settlements

British-aligned First Nation

CREEK

American-aligned First Nation

ONEIDA

The Republic of Vermont,
January 15, 1777–March 4, 1791

Major center of Loyalist activity

100 miles

100km

N

1 2 3 4 5 6 7 8 9 10
11 12 13 14 15 16 17 19 20 21
22 23 24 25 26 27 28 29 30

The Opposing Sides

ORIGINS AND ORGANIZATION

The guerrilla units that operated on both sides during the American Revolutionary War did not evolve in a vacuum. From their inception, the British colonies had an established tradition of communal military obligation that ensured the vast majority of men who served had some preexisting martial training and experience.

In 1775, the Pennsylvania militia was organized under one of the most comprehensive systems in the nation. Its conscription provisions spelled out a table of organization that called for each county to enlist a regiment numbering between 440 and 680 men. Officers were elected, but all colonels and majors had to be property holders and all officers had to be qualified voters. County lieutenants were authorized to hire substitutes to fill the ranks, the cost to be borne by the state, presumably from fines collected from those who wanted to avoid service.

In Tryon County, New York, every male aged 16 to 50 was eligible for militia duty except indentured servants, slaves, the indigenous peoples, and the disabled. Free blacks were expected to serve and slaves were accepted, with the agreement of their owners, often as substitutes for freemen unwilling to face the obligation of service. A few men such as government employees, grist mill and ferry operators, Quakers, and the elderly were granted exemptions, but these could be waived during emergencies. In August 1775, the Provincial Congress ordered those refusing service be fined and the funds generated used to clothe and equip poorer men. By 1776, failing to muster had become a litmus test for concealed disaffection toward the Patriot cause. Such men were not allowed to supply a substitute or pay a fine, but were instead subject to imprisonment or forced service.

Given that the Patriots had by the end of 1775 effective control over all of what were known as the Thirteen Colonies, they inherited the established framework of the existing county militia organizations. These would constitute the backbone of the Patriot resistance for the duration of the war. The British were therefore in the difficult position of having to construct their militias from the ground up, a challenge made even more difficult by the fact that, outside of New York City, they did not retain a stable geographic foundation in the Thirteen Colonies that could provide the basis for institutional loyalty.

Time and again, the British would march into a territory or region, Loyalists would rally to their standard, and then the British would march out again, giving their new auxiliaries the options of either returning to their homes at the mercy of their Patriot neighbors or leaving their families behind and departing for an uncertain future in Crown service. The British captured and occupied Philadelphia in September 1777; when they pulled out in June 1778 they took the Loyalist units they had raised there – the Philadelphia Light Dragoons, the Bucks County Light Dragoons, the Chester County Light Dragoons, the Scottish Volunteers, the Caledonian Volunteers, and the Roman Catholic Volunteers – with them. These men would continue to fight for king and country, but only after the associations they had enlisted in were subsumed into larger companies and dispatched to far-flung fronts amid people to whom they had no connection.

While the Loyalist militias served at the pleasure of the Crown, coordination between the Continental Army and its militias was always a process of protracted negotiation. Brigadier General Richard Montgomery, who commanded the ill-fated invasion of Canada in 1775, professed himself astonished to be "at the head of troops who carry the spirit of freedom into the field, and think for themselves" (quoted in Force 1840: 1375). George Washington, Commanding General of the Continental Army, was perceptive enough to appreciate, "People unused to restraint must be led, they will not be drove" (Founders Online).

Some Continental Army officers, most prominently Major General Nathanael Greene, recognized this, and established an effective and highly productive working relationship with their militia commanders. In the absence of this cooperation, however, the outcome could be disastrous, or even farcical. In the summer of 1778, several backcountry militia units from South Carolina and Georgia accompanied Continental Army troops led by Major General Robert Howe on a campaign to take St. Augustine from the British, but upon reaching Florida, the militia commanders, Brigadier General Andrew Williamson and Governor John Houstoun, refused to put their troops under Howe's command. As a result of this dispute over military authority, the expedition collapsed, its surviving members starving and wracked with disease.

In some instances, the Patriot guerrillas were a law unto themselves. When the Second Continental Congress proved uninterested in his proposal to organize statehood from the New Hampshire Grants, on January 15, 1777, Colonel Ethan Allen and his Green Mountain Boys formed the self-proclaimed Republic of Vermont and opened negotiations with the Crown for recognition. Vermont would not formally enter the Union until March 4, 1791.

During the night of January 24/25, 1783, the Patriots made one last concerted effort to eliminate their nemesis, Lieutenant Colonel James DeLancey, commander of the Loyalist Westchester Light Horse, the infamous Cowboys. This militiaman, sweating and freezing at the same time, is exhausted from marching, fighting, marching again, and then moving through deep drifts of snow for many hours. Now he is trying to quell a sense of panic as the thundering sound of the hooves of Loyalist cavalry horses draws ever nearer. Desperately, he prepares to make a stand to buy enough time for his brothers-in-arms to make good their escape across the frozen Hudson River.

Weapons, dress, and equipment

He is armed with a 17.5mm-caliber 1777 Pattern French Army flintlock musket (**1**), which he has swung up into a firing position.

The Patriot militia that fought the guerrilla war in Westchester County wore no uniform other than the hunting frocks as specified by Washington during the 1776 campaign. The classic Minuteman was indistinguishable from a civilian. This individual wears a classic colonial tricorn hat (**2**) and a cotton shirt, which can just be glimpsed at the collar beneath a linen hunting frock (**3**). On top of this he is wearing a woolen military cloak (**4**) which he has acquired one way or another from a Regular in the Continental Army. Beneath the waist,

he is wearing standard trousers for the era (**5**). On his feet he wears leather shoes (**6**).

His powder horn (**7**) hangs from a leather strap slung over his left shoulder, along with his leather shot pouch (**8**). Note that as a veteran he has had the presence of mind to transfer a number of musket balls from his pocket to his mouth for ease of reloading, hence the bulge in his cheek. His outfit is completed by a wooden canteen (**9**) hanging from another leather strap slung over his right shoulder, and a hatchet (**10**) tucked into his leather belt for close-quarter combat.

MOTIVATIONS AND RECRUITMENT

Because the administrative elite of the colonies was the physical manifestation of British authority, the American Revolution (1765–83) has often been cast in terms of a class struggle, with the scrappy patriotic underdogs – the "people" – rising up to wrest their fundamental rights from an unrepresentative aristocracy. Those constituencies that tended to be identified with loyalism did include officeholders, along with merchants anxious not to lose their trade privileges within the British Empire, and lawyers apprehensive of what revolution would mean for established jurisprudence. If attachment to the Crown was limited to these rarefied circles, however, it would not have factored into the ensuing conflict, whereas the Loyalist contribution to the British war effort was considerable. Between 1775 and 1781 at least 50 distinct provincial corps – some 312 companies – were commissioned. The number of Loyalists under arms increased from 7,500 in December 1778 to nearly 9,000 in December 1779 and over 10,000 in December 1780. More than 15,000 men joined provincial corps at some time during the war, and probably another 10,000 served part-time in a militia unit or a Loyalist association.

Where did these men come from? Loyalists as well as Patriots could be found among the artisans and small farmers who constituted the backbone of colonial society, but, ironically, far from such men representing the political expression of a cultured elite, loyalism was strongest among those who occupied the margins of British North America – immigrants, the indigenous peoples of the First Nations, and the brutalized underclass of enslaved African Americans. Poor backcountry farmers in South Carolina generally preferred the rule of the king to that of the elitist Charleston and lowcountry merchants and plantation owners, who disdained backcountry people and denied them fair representation in the State Assembly.

TEUCRO DUCE NIL DESPERANDUM.

Firft Battalion of PENNSYLVANIA LOYALISTS, commanded by His Excellency Sir WILLIAM HOWE, K. B.

ALL INTREPID ABLE-BODIED

HEROES,

WHO are willing to ferve His MAJESTY KING GEORGE the Third, in Defence of their Country, Laws and Conftitution, againft the arbitrary Ufurpations of a tyrannical Congrefs, have now not only an Opportunity of manifefting their Spirit, by affifting in reducing to Obedience their too-long deluded Countrymen, but alfo of acquiring the polite Accomplifhments of a Soldier, by ferving only two Years, or during the prefent Rebellion in America.

Such fpirited Fellows, who are willing to engage, will be rewarded at the End of the War, befides their Laurels, with 50 Acres of Land, where every gallant Hero may retire, and enjoy his Bottle and Lafs.

Each Volunteer will receive, as a Bounty, FIVE DOLLARS, befides Arms, Cloathing and Accoutrements, and every other Requifite proper to accommodate a Gentleman Soldier, by applying to Lieutenant Colonel ALLEN, or at Captain KEARNY'S Rendezvous, at PATRICK TONRY'S, three Doors above Market-ftreet, in Second-ftreet.

In terms of religious affiliation, Anglicans were bedrock Loyalists while the other denominations – Congregationalists, Presbyterians, Baptists, Lutherans, Dutch Reformed, and Roman Catholics – who shared a common resentment toward the established, tax-supported Anglican Church, all leaned toward independence. The comparatively small number of Jews in America were nearly all Patriots. The Quakers, Mennonites, Moravians, and Amish refused to fight because they believed that war was wrong, and as a consequence were persecuted by both sides. Goaded beyond endurance, many Quakers in Monmouth County, New Jersey, renounced their pacifism and took up arms, at least 36 with the Patriots, and 26 as Loyalists. Some Quakers even banded together to form their own associations, such as the Woodward gang of New Jersey, and the Doan gang of Pennsylvania.

Old grudges within the colonies also helped shape commitments when war broke out on April 19, 1775. In the Carolinas during the 1760s, vigilante groups known as Regulators had been organized to hunt down bandit gangs. The Regulators, in turn, were met by counter-vigilantes known as Moderators. Such blood feuds between neighbors often determined whose side one was on during the war.

British immigrants who arrived in America after the French and Indian War (1754–63) were much more likely to remain loyal than earlier settlers. Established American families were more secure, and hence inclined toward independence. The latecomers, still finding their way in a vast and strange new continent, tended to lean toward Mother England. Scottish Highlanders, for example, though Presbyterian and the subject of ethnic cleansing from their homeland by the Hanoverian monarchs, remained devoted to the Crown because, unlike their Scots-Irish brethren, they were recent immigrants to America who owed their land grants to King George III (r. 1760–1820). The Scottish Highlander Loyalists rallied for the Crown in North Carolina but, when marching to the coast to link up with the British, were bloodily repulsed by a Patriot militia as they attempted to cross Moore's Creek Bridge

No officer who served in the Continental Army better understood how to utilize the full potential of Patriot volunteers than Nathanael Greene. Quartermaster General from 1778 to 1780, he succeeded Major General Horatio Gates with the thankless task of rebuilding Patriot fortunes in the South after the British triumphs at Charleston and Camden (both 1780). From this low ebb he organized a brilliant series of holding actions that kept the main British army frustrated, enabling Patriot militias to undermine Royal authority in a relentless series of small-unit actions. While Greene forged an effective partnership with the irregulars, the nature of partisan warfare in the South dismayed him. "The division among the people is much greater than I imagined and the Whigs and Tories persecute each other, with little less than savage fury," he wrote to Alexander Hamilton; "There is nothing but murders and devastations in every quarter" (Founders Online). (MPI/Getty Images)

on February 27, 1776. The Loyalists in South Carolina had already been suppressed when, falling back to Cherokee territory, they were surprised by a Patriot militia and routed while in camp at Great Cane Brake on the Reedy River on December 22, 1775. Loyalist resistance in the Carolinas was rendered inert by these defeats, and would not revive until the arrival of Lieutenant-General Sir Henry Clinton with the main British Army in the spring of 1780.

It was a similar story in Virginia, where Royal Governor Lord Dunmore issued a proclamation on November 7, 1775, declaring "all indented servants, negroes, or others (appertaining to rebels) free" (quoted in Moore 1908: 6). Hundreds of runaways flocked to enlist in Dunmore's Ethiopian Regiment, but after this unit, alongside white Loyalists and Regular infantry, was decisively defeated by Patriot militia at the battle of Great Bridge on December 9, 1775, British authority in Virginia evaporated. The British did not consider the appeal to enslaved persons a dead end, however. From his Philipsburg headquarters in Westchester County, New York, on June 30, 1779, Clinton issued a proclamation promising every enslaved person who left Patriot service "full security" from re-enslavement and their choice of "any Occupation which he shall think proper" (quoted in Moore 1908: 20) in British service. Tens of thousands of fugitives would seek refuge behind British lines during the course of the war.

The Patriots struggled throughout the war to reconcile their practical need for manpower with their devotion to racial hierarchy. Younger and more idealistic Patriots, like Lieutenant Colonel Alexander Hamilton and Lieutenant Colonel John Laurens, vigorously advocated for emancipation as a logical and necessary corollary of the struggle for freedom – but the entrenched interests of the Southern plantation aristocrats proved too powerful to overcome. Notwithstanding the institutional hostility to their interests, many African Americans elected to serve the Patriot cause in some capacity, and with distinction. Jim Capers, a free black man who served as a drum major under another Patriot militia commander, Brigadier General Francis Marion, suffered multiple wounds during the battle of Eutaw Springs on September 8, 1781.

Most First Nations elected to retain their established relationships with the British on a better-the-devil-you know basis, although there were important exceptions, such as the Oneida and Tuscarora in the north and Catawba in the south, who sided with the Patriots. From the beginning, the British sought to utilize the indigenous peoples as a means to keep the rebellious colonists in line. British alliances with the First Nations were included as grievances against the King listed in the Declaration of Independence published on July 4, 1776: "He has endeavored to bring on the inhabitants of our frontiers, the merciless Indian savages."

Geographic location played an important part in determining allegiances. Britain's possessions in Canada, to the north of the Thirteen Colonies, and Florida, to the south, were steadfast in their attachment to the Crown, providing both safe refuge for Loyalist refugees and jumping-off points for incursions into Patriot territory.

By contrast, overt loyalty to the Crown throughout the Thirteen Colonies became increasingly hazardous as British authority waned. In addition to their program of nation building based on moral suasion and nascent civic identity, the Patriots were prepared to use more overt methods to impose a consensus behind independence. In the Hudson Valley, New York, a Commission for Detecting and Defeating Conspiracies engaged in a zealous campaign to root out the recalcitrant in the region. Meeting alternately in Fishkill, Poughkeepsie, Rhinebeck, and Kingston, authorities arrested hundreds of suspected traitors for assault, conspiracy, desertion, espionage, murder, providing aid and comfort to the enemy, theft, and other criminal or seditious activities; and yet, more men from New York would ultimately serve in Loyalist regiments than in the Continental Army. As the English-born American political activist Thomas Paine lamented when the British brought their full force against New York City in August 1776, "Why is it that the enemy hath left the New-England provinces and made these middle ones the seat of war? The answer is easy: New-England is not infested with Tories, and we are" (Paine 1817: 53).

Maryland was split by Chesapeake Bay; Patriots predominated in the tobacco-growing western counties, while the maritime Eastern Shore was Loyalist. Monmouth County, New Jersey, was bitterly divided; it can be conservatively estimated that two-thirds of the male population took up arms on one side or the other during the war, 605 serving in the New Jersey Volunteers – roughly 30 percent of the total number of enrollees in what was the largest Loyalist corps raised in the Thirteen Colonies, and more than 10 percent of Monmouth County's adult male population.

Within the Thirteen Colonies, whole communities, neighborhoods, even individual families – the nucleus of any functioning society – could be split irrevocably by the divisions of war. Those related by blood could find each other, inadvertently or otherwise, on opposite sides during a battle. When 28-year-old Brigadier General George Rogers Clark campaigned against the First Nations of the Ohio River Valley during the summer of 1780, among the casualties when his militia stormed the village of Piqua on August 8 was his 25-year-old cousin Joseph Rogers, who had been kidnapped by the Shawnee years earlier and adopted into the tribe.

On both sides, the motivations for enlistment might vary from genuine ideological commitment to filial obligation or personal grievance. Pecuniary opportunity was a primary inducement, and both sides were generous in pledging rewards to their partisans, to be taken from the loser after a successful conclusion to the war, as an inducement toward victory. Typically, in addition to five dollars in bounty, men who enlisted in the Loyalist Royal American Volunteers were promised 100 acres of tax-free land on the Mississippi.

Throughout the war, there was no shortage of Loyalist volunteers for service with the Crown, but these men tended to be exiles and refugees who, once mobilized, could find themselves serving in units dispatched to theaters of operation far from their original homes. A critical distinction between Patriot and Loyalist militias, therefore, is that the former always fought in and for their own communities and possessed the priceless gift of intimate local knowledge, whereas the latter might be serving the strategic interests of the Crown in an environment and amid a population where they were almost as alien as the Redcoats they fought alongside.

This German illustration depicts a Patriot rifleman (left) and a musket-armed Pennsylvanian infantryman. The British could take the great cities of the eastern seaboard – New York, Philadelphia, Charleston – but, confronted by an opponent that melted away into the interior of the continent to regroup, found themselves at a strategic dead end, lacking both the manpower to pacify the surrounding countryside and a message that could win over the hearts and minds of its inhabitants. "The inclinations of the Americans, though averse from tactical arrangement," Lieutenant-Colonel John Graves Simcoe observed, were ideally suited to the protracted guerrilla struggle that ensued, for "the Indians, their original enemies, and the nature of their country, had familiarized them to this species of warfare, and they were, in general, excellent marksmen" (Simcoe 1844: 95). (Fotosearch/Getty Images)

Dragoon, Westchester Light Horse

This cavalryman is a typical Cowboy, one of those Loyalist refugees exiled from their communities who were rallied and raised as a military force by DeLancey to contest control of Westchester County with the Patriots. If there was time, the dragoon might halt to dismount and shoot it out with the militia, but having surprised his enemy on open ground, he is charging with drawn saber.

Weapons, dress, and equipment

His saber (**1**) features a brass and iron mounted hilt fitted to a 25in-long, slightly curved, single-edged, plain blade with a rounded point. The one-piece grip is crafted from wood carved in a spiral pattern, with a brass hilt and brass base attached. His primary firearm, a .65-caliber 1773 British Elliot Dragoon flintlock carbine (**2**), is attached to his right-hand cross belt, its muzzle facing downward and inserted into a bucket (**3**) that connects to the saddle for stability while on the gallop.

His helmet is modeled on that worn by another Loyalist light cavalry unit, Lieutenant-Colonel Banastre Tarleton's notorious British Legion. Fashioned from hardened leather, its scuffed carapace (**4**) is bound by a cloth headband (**5**) and topped by a formidable bearskin crest (**6**). He wears a white waistcoat beneath a green uniform coat (**7**) that terminates in black cuffs and collar. His legs are clad in off-white riding breeches (**8**), which are tucked into riding boots with spurs (**9**).

Two cross belts (**10**) are slung over the coat. His leather scabbard (**11**) has a brass drag mounted at its tip and a brass top band with its single brass hook for securing to his left-hand cross belt. His regulation shot pouch (**12**) is attached to his waist belt and tucked into his abdomen for ease of access.

His mount wears a standard British Elliot 1759 light dragoon saddle (**13**), strapped into place on top of a horse blanket (**14**). Behind the saddle is the trooper's bedroll (**15**). Two pistol holsters are slung on either side of the saddle in front of the rider, both of them almost hidden beneath the fur ruff (**16**) in front of the saddle. The holsters contain a pair of brass .62-caliber Elliot Light Dragoon flintlock pistols. On a standard raid, his mount might carry additional gear, but on an urgent interception mission like this, the dragoon would be traveling light.

Soldiers on garrison duty, especially over the long winter months, will often keep their minds active by personalizing their gear with decorations or mnemonics. The contemporary powder horn on the left is engraved with scenes of men dueling and hunting, the royal arms of Great Britain, and a map of the settlements in Cherokee territory. To the Patriots, the Cherokee, who had responded to British inducement by launching raids along the frontier, represented an existential threat on their western flank. Patriot militias under Major Andrew Williamson and Major Andrew Pickens waged a brutal campaign against the Cherokee, who were forced under the terms of the May 20, 1777 Treaty of DeWitt's Corner to cede all their remaining territory in South Carolina. The horn on the right is engraved with the name of its owner, Peter Myer; the British coat of arms; and a map of the forts in the Hudson and Mohawk valleys, control over which was critical to strategists on both sides as they were the primary trade – and invasion – routes linking the Thirteen Colonies to Canada. By the end of the war, incessant British, Loyalist, and First Nations incursions had left these borderlands burned-out and depopulated. (metmuseum.org/CC0 1.0)

OPPOSITE
Other than specialist units, Loyalists and their First Nations allies were armed with the British establishment Brown Bess musket, either in the older Long Land Service Pattern (overall length 62½in) or – depicted here – the newer Short Land Service Pattern (overall length 58½in), both of which could be fitted with a 17in triangular cross-section bayonet. (MPI/Getty Images)

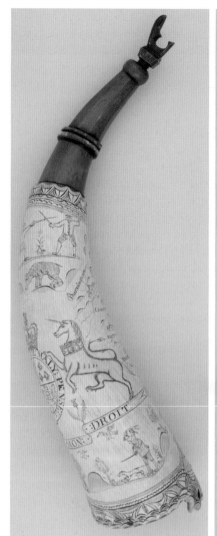 

WEAPONS, GEAR, AND TERMS OF SERVICE

A major distinction between Loyalist and Patriot militias was that while the former would, as soon as possible, be processed into units with standardized uniforms, weapons, and equipment, the latter never were. Therefore, if the two sides clashed prior to the Loyalists being so organized, they would be virtually indistinguishable. Simple markers of identity could be resorted to, such as specific colors of paper or variants of flora displayed in hats, but in the confusion of nonlinear guerrilla warfare, friendly-fire incidents were an unavoidable hazard. On February 25, 1781, a 400-strong band of local Loyalist volunteers under Dr. John Pyle marching to link up with Lieutenant-General Charles, Lord Cornwallis fell in with a green-coated company of cavalry they were led to believe was Lieutenant-Colonel Banastre Tarleton's British Legion. In fact, the horsemen were Continental Army dragoons under Lieutenant Colonel Henry "Light Horse Harry" Lee. When fighting erupted, the bewildered Loyalists were slaughtered.

While there was little expectation of regularity in Patriot militia service, units tended to operate within the same parameters throughout the colonies, with a long-established emphasis on functionality. Tryon County, New York, regulations mandated that each man was to provide a firelock in good working order with a steel ramrod, a cleaning worm, 12 spare flints, and a tool to fix and knap them. In reality, when the militia mustered in 1777 there would have been a few decent rifles and smoothbores and many poorer ones, from hunting pieces to castoffs and heirlooms from wars long past. Many militiamen carried a large cow horn to contain the mandated amount of coarse main-charge powder and a smaller one with fine priming powder. These men used a leather bag to carry the prescribed 23 musket balls and wadding. Others had the preferred cartridge pouch with prepared paper cartridges, as used by Regulars.

There were few if any bayonets on the frontier, but every man was equipped with some form of edged weapon, typically a hunting knife or tomahawk. Officers bore swords or a half-pike called a spontoon. Everyone in the rank and file brought a canteen and perhaps a tin cup for drinking water, a blanket for bedding, and a haversack containing sufficient rations (bread, cheese, and cooked or smoke-cured meats) for three days of marching. The men tasked with relieving Fort Stanwix were to remain there in garrison, so they brought with them an extra shirt and stockings, a spoon, a sheath or clasp knife, a bowl or plate, and soap and shaving kit. Only a handful would have been in uniforms from previous service, perhaps from the failed invasion of Canada two years earlier. Most turned out in their well-worn everyday clothes, the majority being farmers in hunting shirts, work smocks, waistcoats, jackets, and linsey-woolsey (linen and wool, or cotton and wool) or leather breeches, the earthen hues serendipitously offering camouflage. As was the custom, every man would wear some form of hat.

Sixteen-year-old James Collins, a veteran of many campaigns in the turbulent partisan warfare that engulfed South Carolina in 1780, described his Patriot guerrilla band as being composed entirely of volunteers acting on their own recognizance, "without the promise or expectation of any pay" (Collins 1859: 32). The men rode in on their own horses, with saddles, bridles, and other equipage, down to the spurs, provided at their own expense. Firearms, too, were derived from personal collections. Maintaining stocks of gunpowder was a constant worry, and the guerrillas often had to solicit homesteading women for their old pewter dishes and cutlery in lieu of lead. Local manufacturing also met the need for close-quarter weapons, as Patriot blacksmiths were accomplished in processing scrap metal into swords and knives. Always precariously balanced between opportunity before them and danger behind, the Patriots treaded lightly. They carried no baggage, no cooking utensils, or anything else that might encumber their movement, Collins recalled; "we depended on what chance or kind providence might cast in our way" (Collins 1859: 36), hunting and foraging, always on the move, ready to break camp at a moment's notice.

The British had not been slow to recruit volunteers from among their still-loyal subjects in the colonies. The Queen's Rangers, raised and commanded by Lieutenant-Colonel Robert Rogers, had seen service during the White Plains campaign of Major-General William Howe, commander-in-chief of British

A reenactor – clad in the costume of the previous generation, fighting the French and Indian War (1754–63) – fills the flash pan of a replica muzzle-loading flintlock firearm (left) before firing it (right). Although slow to reload, the firearms of the era had one significant advantage over their modern-day equivalents in that their owners were not entirely dependent on finite stocks of industrially manufactured ammunition but could improvise their own. (DEA/C. BALOSSINI/Getty Images)

OPPOSITE
A .69-caliber French musket, c.1779. Throughout the war the Patriots were forced to make do with a miscellany of firearms, including Pennsylvania or Kentucky Long Rifles, Brown Bess muskets liberated from their owners, an assortment of domestically manufactured variants of the Brown Bess, or other models imported from overseas, such as the 1766 Pattern French Army Musket, the Spanish M1752 Musket, and the Prussian 1740 Pattern Potsdam Musket. (NPI/Getty Images)

land forces in North America, taking significant casualties in a skirmish at Heathcote Hill, Mamaroneck, on October 22, 1776. To replenish the ranks of his unit, on December 30, 1776, Rogers authorized recruitment on the following terms:

> No more than forty shillings bounty is to be given to any man, which is to be applied toward purchasing necessities; to serve during the present rebellion and no longer. They will have their proportion of all rebel lands, and all privileges equal to any of his Majesty's troops. The officers are to be the best judges in what manner they will get their men in, either by parties, detachments, or other wise, as may seem most advantageous. (Quoted in Cutter 1861: 373)

In New York, Westchester County estate owner Beverley Robinson raised the Loyal American Regiment and served as its colonel. Frederick Philipse III, who owned Philipsburgh Manor, was interred on August 9, 1776, by the Patriots on the orders of Washington and spent six months in a Connecticut prison before taking his wife and nine children into the British lines; five of his sons would fight for the Crown. Another member of the landed elite, Colonel William Bayard, also fled to New York City and raised a battalion of troops, the King's Orange Rangers, in which two of his sons were officers.

The officers who served in the Westchester Refugees under Lieutenant Colonel James DeLancey in Westchester County were typically drawn from the elite strata of society, men like James Hunt and Samuel Kipp. As gentlemen of independent means operating outside of the regular military establishment, the officers of DeLancey's 500-strong corps, stationed at Morrisania, were able to relieve some of the financial pressure imposed on the Royal treasury by the burden of occupation and war, serving unpaid and, if mounted, without compensation for the foraging or maintenance of their horses. Kipp asserted the unit, which held the front line in New York throughout the entire war, did so without any remuneration save the satisfaction of doing their duty as faithful subjects (Tiedemann et al. 2010: 119).

DOCTRINE AND TACTICS

George Washington held a low opinion of the militia at the beginning of the war: "To place any dependence upon Militia, is assuredly, resting upon a broken staff," he insisted to John Hancock, President of the Second Continental Congress, on September 25, 1776; "unaccustomed to the din of Arms; totally unacquainted with every kind of Military skills, when opposed by Troops regularly train'd, disciplined and appointed, makes them timid and ready to fly at their own shadows" (Founders Online). On August 16, 1780, when the Patriot militia disintegrated during the battle of Camden, he was even more convinced than ever his judgment was correct. Colonel Otho Holland Williams of the 6th Maryland Regiment described the British bayonet charge, which "threw the whole body of the militia into such a panic that they generally threw down their *loaded* arms and fled in the utmost consternation" (quoted in Johnson 1822: 495). It was a similar story at the battle of Guilford Courthouse on March 15, 1781, where, despite suffering no casualties, "To our infinite distress and mortification, the North Carolina militia took to flight," Lee lamented; every effort by the officers "to stop this unaccountable panic" was "in vain," as, abandoning everything, "they rushed like a torrent through the woods" (Lee 1827: 172–73).

These assessments, while accurate, were unfair, for the militia was being tasked in each instance with a responsibility it was not fit for. By definition, irregular troops were intended for nonlinear, guerrilla warfare, not as line units in a conventional battle. Washington emphasized this fact to his subordinates, that they must not expect from the militia "services for which Regulars alone are fit" (Founders Online).

Where the militia came into its own was in the roles of reconnaissance and intelligence gathering, harassment of enemy supply lines, suppression of enemy recruitment, and counterinsurgency – preventing the militia on the other side from doing precisely the same things. On this basis, sometimes as adjuncts to strategic initiatives undertaken by the regular armies, sometimes through pursuing tactical opportunities on their own initiative, Patriot irregulars and Loyalist associations fought out a multitude of small-unit actions that could range from a few dozen men to as many as several hundred on each side.

Loyalist refugees stationed on Long Island, New York, engaged in a bitter contest of raid and counterraid across Long Island Sound throughout the war. Loyalists staged their incursions against New Jersey primarily from four stations: Staten Island, Fort Delancey (on Bergen Neck), Bull's Ferry (opposite Manhattan), and Refugeetown at Sandy Hook, the last of these having been founded in 1778 by fugitive African American slaves and poor white Loyalist refugees. On May 9, 1779, Loyalists burned most of the houses and barns in the village of Closter in Bergen County, New Jersey. Patriots killed at least one of the raiders; they stripped his corpse and strung it up with a placard warning, "No quarter to refugees." Undeterred, in the summer of 1780, white and black Loyalists attacked the old Huguenot community of Schraalenburgh, reducing it to rubble.

Loyalist freebooters based on Staten Island included Cornelius Hatfield, Jr., and Nathaniel Robbins. One of the most important Loyalist partisans to

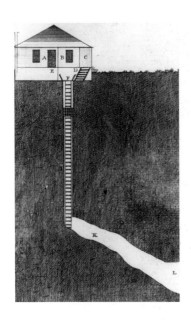

Prospects for incarcerated partisans on both sides during the war were grim. Patriots faced being consigned to British prison barges rotting at the wharves of New York Harbor while Loyalists might be condemned to Newgate Prison, formerly the Simsbury Mine, an old copper mine in East Granby, Connecticut. The mine was some 60ft underground, the only entrance being via a ladder down a narrow shaft into the total darkness of the reeking, waterlogged, vermin-ridden interior. With nothing to lose, the 28 Loyalists imprisoned here staged a desperate breakout on May 18, 1781, seizing control of the guardhouse and herding their erstwhile jailors underground in their place before locking the hatch and fleeing into the night. (Library of Congress)

use Staten Island as a base for banditry and commissioned military operations was a fugitive slave from Monmouth County, New Jersey, named Titus, who had run away from the farm of John Corlies in Colts Neck along the Navesink River near the town of Shrewsbury in Monmouth County. Titus had heard about Lord Dunmore's proclamation in November 1775 and joined the British military as a means to gain his freedom permanently. Because of Titus' gallantry at the battle of Monmouth on June 28, 1778, the British Army bestowed on him the ceremonial title of "Colonel Tye." Tye learned to navigate the Navesink River and gained knowledge of the property, wealth, commodities, and political leanings of the families in the area. Accordingly, he became an invaluable source of information for the British regarding Monmouth County's topography, residents, and forage.

The British encouraged African American refugees into forming provincial corps, or even actively organized them as such, examples being the Jamaica Volunteers and the Negro Horse. In Charleston, South Carolina, Lieutenant-Colonel Benjamin Thompson, a New Hampshire Loyalist, drilled a unit of cavalry Patriots dubbed the Black Dragoons. These units sometimes incorporated entire families. Captain George Martin of the Royal Marines organized fugitive slaves into the Black Pioneers, which in August 1780 listed 182 men, 74 women, and 73 children on its roll. Tye was one of the African Americans – 49 men, 23 women, and six children – at Refugeetown who organized themselves into the Black Brigade. During a series of raids into Monmouth County that commenced on July 15, 1779, this unit carried off valuables and badly needed foodstuffs, horses, and cattle for the British forces on Staten Island and in New York City, liberated many slaves, and captured prominent Patriots, including two members of the State Assembly.

On the evening of August 31, 1780, Tye led a mixed-race party of about 30 men and penetrated 15 miles inland to the tavern of Joshua Huddy at Colts Neck. Huddy, who had been granted a privateer's commission by the Second Continental Congress, was targeted for his raids on Staten Island and Refugeetown, and for executing Loyalist prisoners, including the hanging of Stephen Edwards. Near dawn, Tye's men surrounded the tavern, but Huddy and his mistress, Lucretia Emmons, successfully held off the raiders until the building was put to the torch. The sun was up by the time the Black Brigade made it back to shore, where they were intercepted by detachments of Salem and Monmouth County militia. In the ensuing skirmish, Huddy was shot in the leg, but succeeded in swimming to safety. Tye was shot through the wrist in this encounter; he contracted tetanus and died some time later. His boldness and vigor commanded respect even from his enemies; the Patriot *New-Jersey Gazette* eulogized Tye as particularly courageous, making the explicit point that he was more highly regarded among his Patriot foes than his white Loyalist counterparts (Gilbert & Gilbert 2015: 148).

Tye was succeeded by "Colonel" Stephen Bleuke, a freeborn volunteer from Barbados, and the incursions continued. On October 17, 1781, Patriot militia Colonel Nathaniel Scudder was killed in a skirmish with Loyalist raiders. A doctor and former President of the Medical Society of New Jersey,

Scudder had been elected to the New Jersey General Assembly and the Second Continental Congress; he was the only member of that body killed in action during the course of the war, and the last colonel to die before the war ended.

Where the British had a permanent presence, Loyalists were proactive, striking south from Canada, north from Florida, and outward from New York City. This put them on at least equal terms with their Patriot rivals, and it was in these theaters that Loyalists enjoyed greatest success. Conversely, in territory occupied by the British while on campaign, the Loyalists were expected to operate in a policing role to hold the ground claimed while the regular army proceeded ahead to the next objective. In this environment, however, Loyalists tended to be on the back foot, reacting to Patriot initiatives. Writing after the war, Tarleton's deputy, Major George Hanger, identified the persistent tactical dilemma that confronted the British: "… militia in those parts of America are all mounted on horseback, which renders it totally impossible to force them to an engagement with infantry only" (Hanger 1789: 82). When they elected to fight, the Patriots would dismount and fasten their horses to fences and rails in order to secure their line and method of retreat; but, if not convinced they had had established local superiority, "they remain on horseback, give their fire, and retreat, which renders it useless to attack them without cavalry: for though you repulse them and drive them from the field, you can never improve the advantage, or do them material detriment" (Hanger 1789: 82). Although hard-riding counterthrusts by the likes of Lieutenant-Colonel John Graves Simcoe, DeLancey, and Tarleton himself might temporarily redress this imbalance, their exploits ultimately only succeeded in alienating the communities in which they operated. It was the Patriots who understood this political aspect of the struggle for American independence, and that understanding established the foundations of their victory.

Westchester County

1776–83

BACKGROUND TO BATTLE

Westchester was caught up in the escalating confrontation with Great Britain during the 1770s, which exposed widening and increasingly irreconcilable differences between the Patriots and Loyalists. On April 11, 1775, hundreds of the latter gathered at Hatfield's Tavern, in White Plains: "We are met here to express our honest abhorrence of all unlawful Congresses and Committees, and that we are determined at the hazard of our lives and property, to support the King and Constitution" (Moore 1876: 62).

In response, in a circular issued April 27 the New York Committee of Inspection called for a Provincial Congress to assemble at White Plains.

Meeting on May 8, this body elected 12 members to the Provincial Congress of New York, which the Continental Congress called on to raise four regiments of Continental Line in Westchester County. In August, the Provincial Congress passed a bill providing New York be divided into districts, each of which was to be capable of raising 83 men between 16 and 60 years of age, able to bear arms; these were to be formed into companies, and permitted to elect their own officers. Every man was to provide himself with a musket and bayonet, a sword or tomahawk, a cartridge box to contain 23 rounds of ammunition, a knapsack, 1lb of gunpowder, 12 flints, and 3lb of balls to fit his gun. One-quarter of them were to be organized as Minutemen.

Under this order, 28 companies of militia were organized in Westchester County, commanded by Colonels Joseph Drake, James Hammond, Thomas Thomas, and Pierre Van Cortlandt. Eight of these companies, from the Manor of Cortlandt, formed the North Battalion. The Middle Battalion of 11 companies consisted of one from Rye and Mamaroneck, one from Harrison, two from North Castle, one from Scarsdale, White Plains, and Brown's Point, two from Bedford, one from Pound Ridge, and two from North and South Salem. The South Battalion consisted of one company from Yonkers, one from Eastchester, one from New Rochelle and Pelham, and five from Philipsburgh, plus two unattached companies.

Those assuming leadership roles emerged organically from within the communities as they mustered. William Dutcher, a well-respected community leader, was elected captain of the Upper Philipsburgh Associated Company of Militia, a command consisting of roughly 30 men, including a first lieutenant, second lieutenant, three sergeants, two drummers and a fifer. One loose association of individuals who would prove vital to the Patriot cause during the long years of conflict were the trackers and scouts dubbed the Westchester Guides. Prominent individuals included the brothers Abraham and Michael Dyckman of Kingsbridge, Cornelius Oakley of White Plains, and John Odell of Cortlandt.

MAP KEY

1 August 28, 1776: The first clash between Patriots and Loyalists occurs at Mamaroneck.

2 October 22, 1776: Protecting the right flank of the British army as it advances north, the Queen's Rangers are ambushed in a late-evening assault at Heathcote Hill, Mamaroneck, losing 21 killed or wounded and 36 prisoners.

3 October 28, 1776: In the battle of White Plains, Washington and the main American Army are driven out of Westchester County.

4 March 16, 1777: Loyalists raid detachments of the Dutchess County and Westchester County militias at Ward's House, killing six and taking 27 prisoners.

5 August 31, 1778: Loyalists under Lieutenant-Colonel John Graves Simcoe rout the Patriots at Woodlawn Heights. The Stockbridge First Nation is hard hit, losing 37 killed.

6 September 16, 1778: Loyalists under Simcoe defeat the Patriot force holding the bridge over the Saw Mill River, taking 35 prisoners.

7 December 25, 1778: Loyalists raid Young's House, capturing Joseph Young along with some of the militia present, and driving off the cattle.

8 July 2, 1779: Loyalists under Lieutenant-Colonel Banastre Tarleton rout Colonel Elisha Sheldon's 2nd Continental Light Dragoons and raid Pound Ridge and Bedford.

9 August 5, 1779: Patriots raid Morrisania, Simcoe's riposte evolving into a running fight through Mamaroneck.

10 November 13, 1779: Patriots raid the Archer House in a bid to capture Loyalist Lieutenant Colonel James DeLancey at his quarters.

11 January 17, 1780: Patriots raid Morrisania, taking Loyalist Lieutenant Colonel Isaac Hatfield and another 14 officers and men captive. Loyalist Major Thomas Huggerford escapes and mobilizes a counterattack, which catches up with the Patriot rearguard on its retreat between New Rochelle and Mamaroneck, killing 23 and taking 40 prisoners.

12 February 3, 1780: Loyalists under DeLancey participate in a major raid on Young's House.

13 May 22, 1780: Loyalists raid Horseneck, taking 37 prisoners.

14 September 23, 1780: Three Patriot militiamen capture Major John André just north of Tarrytown, foiling Benedict Arnold's plot to betray West Point and George Washington to the British.

15 December 9, 1780: Loyalists under Huggerford raid Horseneck, capturing a lieutenant colonel, a captain, two lieutenants, two ensigns, and upwards of 20 rank and file.

16 January 22, 1781: A mixed force of Patriots and Continentals raids Morrisania, taking 52 prisoners, and fighting off a British counterattack as it withdraws via Eastchester.

17 May 14, 1781: Loyalists under DeLancey ford the Croton River and raid the headquarters of the 1st Rhode Island Regiment at Yorktown Presbyterian Church, killing 30, including Colonel Christopher Greene. They withdraw via Pines Bridge after routing the garrison stationed there.

18 July 22, 1781: Loyalists are driven out of Morrisania and forced to take refuge on British ships offshore by a combined Patriot and French expeditionary force.

19 December 2, 1781: Patriots repulse a Loyalist raid on Harrison.

20 January 11, February 26, and March 3, 1782: As the tide of war turns, emboldened Patriots stage a succession of raids on Morrisania.

21 January 25, 1783: Patriots raid West Farms in a bid to capture DeLancey. The Loyalist counterattack catches up with the retreating Patriots between Sing Sing and Van Cortlandt, driving the survivors across the ice of the Hudson River.

Battlefield environment

Adjoining the metropolis of New York City to its north, Westchester County was a prosperous agricultural community at the outset of the war. Bounded by the Hudson River to the west and Long Island Sound to the east, the county was dotted with small villages linked by rough local roads and two major arteries, the Boston Post Road to the east, and the Albany Post Road, which crossed over the Williams Bridge and King's Bridge into Manhattan, to the west. The total population was about 28,000 people (24,000 white and 4,000 black, mostly slaves).

While the Continental Army line in Westchester County stretched from Peekskill on the Hudson River then eastward via the Croton River to Mamaroneck on Long Island Sound, the militia adopted a forward posture, with lines radiating from New Rochelle in the east to Yonkers in the west. To the south, the British outer lines extended from Philipse Manor on the Hudson River to Eastchester, supported by outposts at Kingsbridge (which connected the upper tip of Manhattan Island with the mainland), Fordham, West Farms, and Morrisania.

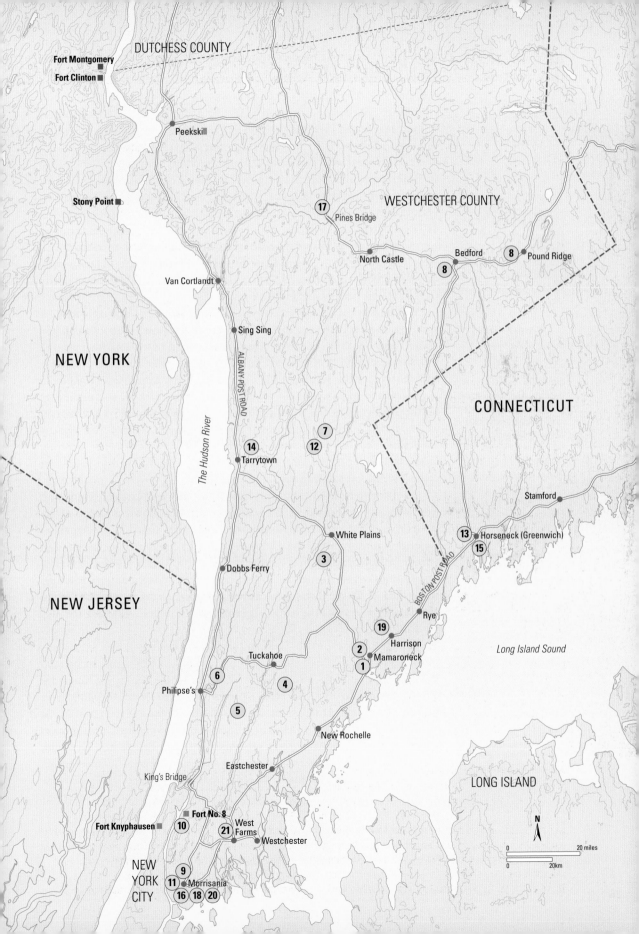

INTO COMBAT

The first blood in Westchester County was shed on August 28, 1776, when the militia surprised and attacked a meeting of 14 Loyalists at Mamaroneck, killing their leader, William Lounsberry, who had a warrant to enlist men for Colonel Robert Rogers' Rangers. The following day, Major-General William Howe's forces defeated the main American army under Washington in Brooklyn. Howe subsequently pushed Washington out of Manhattan, and then defeated him in battle at White Plains in Westchester County on October 28. Washington's victories at Trenton and Princeton in December 1776 stabilized the situation for the Patriots, and the war settled into an uneasy standoff. Washington established his headquarters at Morristown, New Jersey, delegating command of the northern front first to Major General William Heath and then to Major General Alexander McDougall, who established his headquarters at Peekskill.

The British had not been slow to recruit volunteers from among their still-loyal subjects in the colonies. With much of Westchester County now under Patriot control, however, many Loyalists had no option other than to seek shelter behind British lines. The commanding general in New York City, Sir Henry Clinton, stationed the Queen's Rangers, from May 1777 under the command of Lieutenant-Colonel John Graves Simcoe, at Kingsbridge on the Harlem River to guard the main northern approach to Manhattan. On July 18, Clinton appointed his adjutant general, Lord William Shaw Cathcart, to colonel and command of the British Legion. Banastre Tarleton, formerly a major in the 16th Light Dragoons, was promoted to lieutenant colonel of this unit on August 1.

Loyalist refugees converging on New York were organized into numerous units, including Emmerick's Chasseurs and Dragoons, a corps of six companies of infantry and two troops of light dragoons under Lieutenant Colonel Andreas Emmerick; DeLancey's Brigade, under Brigadier General Oliver DeLancey; the Loyal American Regiment, under Colonel Beverley Robinson; the King's American Regiment, under Colonel Edmund Fanning; the Prince of Wales' Royal American Volunteers, under Brigadier-General Montfort Browne; and the King's Orange Rangers, under Lieutenant Colonel John Bayard.

The most prominent – and notorious – Loyalist, James DeLancey, was a nephew of Oliver DeLancey and scion of a family that had boasted immense landholdings and political influence in the colony of New York for generations. In 1770, DeLancey had been elected sheriff of Westchester County and captain of the county militia's Troop of Horse at the age of 23. At the outbreak of the war, however, he refused to break with the Crown and was subject to house arrest. DeLancey subsequently fled to British-held New York City, where New York's Royal Governor, Lieutenant-General William Tryon, placed him in charge of raising Loyalist militia in Westchester County. He was quickly promoted from captain to lieutenant colonel, but in November 1777, he was captured by a Patriot scouting party. Incarcerated in Hartford, Connecticut, he was eventually paroled back to the British, but not without significant misgivings, New York Governor George Clinton noting: "De Lancey is a very bad name" in Patriot circles (Clinton III.355).

DeLancey's militia was derisively dubbed the Cowboys by embittered Patriots for its role in requisitioning – by any means necessary – beef cattle for the British cause from farms the length and breadth of Westchester County and even neighboring Connecticut. At their peak, Cowboy raids supplied one-third of the provisions for the New York City market. Such forays also demoralized and intimidated Patriot communities while enabling the refugees, who served without pay, to compensate themselves for their services and the loss of their estates and livelihoods. In a typical operation in January 1779, the Cowboys seized grain and flour in White Plains and carried off the entire store in 37 wagons. In November 1780, a detachment of Cowboys, 30 mounted and 20 on foot, under Captain Timothy Knapp and Lieutenant James Kipp, seized and drove off 120 head of cattle from Tarrytown.

The fluid tactical environment left the combatants in Westchester County constantly living on a knife edge. DeLancey, public enemy number one for the Patriots, slept in a different house every night to avoid detection and recapture. In March 1781, Patriot physician Dr. James Thacher observed that the situation of those living between the lines was "truly deplorable, being continually exposed to the ravages of tories, horse thieves, and cow boys, who rob and plunder them without mercy, and the personal abuse and punishments which they inflict is almost incredible" (Thacher 1827: 250).

Inevitably, this guerrilla conflict between members of what had been the same communities devolved into brutality and inhumanity. Further coarsening the conflict, while many Loyalists served as uniformed auxiliaries under the aegis of the British, others elected to operate as independent freebooters. These so-called Skinners amounted to little more than opportunistic bandits, taking advantage of the fog of war to plunder and despoil at will.

On the evening of March 16, 1777, the British sent a strong detachment of Regulars, Hessians, and the Queen's Rangers under Captain John Branden and Captain Archibald Campbell to surprise the Americans at Ward's House, composed of a company of Dutchess County militia under Major Brinton Pain and a company of Westchester County militia under Captain Samuel Delavan. Of the Americans, six were killed and 27 captured. The British lost Campbell and five privates killed, and six wounded, one fatally.

In March 1778, Emmerick ordered a cattle raid by 32 men under Lieutenant Althaus against the property of Joseph Young. His son, Samuel Young, was chopping wood about one-quarter mile from the house when he was alerted to the presence of the Loyalists. He ran to find militia sergeant John Dean, who instructed him to run to Dean's home to arm himself while Dean rallied the militia. Young proceeded to Dean's house, where Dean's wife handed him three muskets and two bunches of cartridges. The militia took up a position behind a stone wall along the road Althaus was taking in returning to King's Bridge. The Loyalists were permitted to approach within about 50yd before the ambush was sprung. After a running fight of 4 miles, the Patriots succeeded in killing or taking Althaus and all his men. The Loyalists had their revenge on Christmas night of the same year, storming Young's House and capturing Joseph Young himself, along with some of the militia present, and driving off the cattle. About 20 of the militia escaped into the winter darkness, but some were so afflicted by frostbite they could make no further contribution to the Patriot cause.

On the morning of August 31, Simcoe assembled approximately 500 Loyalists under the command of Tarleton and Emmerick and with them marched up to Woodlawn Heights, on the boundary between Yonkers and Mount Vernon. The American force in the area was a little over 100 strong, half of whom were Native Americans, including members of the Stockbridge First Nation, attached to a newly formed Light Infantry Corps commanded by Colonel Mordecai Gist of Maryland.

Simcoe hoped to entice the Americans forward down Mile Square Road from their positions. At the same time, he would divide his own forces in an effort to envelop and trap the Americans. Emmerick's corps was to take up a position westerly of Tibbet's Brook and Mile Square Road near the residence of a Frederick De Voe, while the Queen's Rangers moved up along the Bronx River; both units were hidden from the Americans by the natural fall of the land. Simcoe described the ensuing action:

> The Queen's Rangers moved rapidly to gain the heights, and Lieut.-Col. Tarleton immediately advanced with the Hussars and the Legion cavalry; not being able to pass the [stone] fences in his front, he made a circuit to return upon their right, which being reported to Lieut.-Col. Simcoe, he broke from the column of the Rangers, with the Grenadier Company, and directed Major Ross to conduct the Corps to the heights, advanced to the road, and arrived without being perceived within ten yards of the Indians, who had been intent upon the attack of Emmerick's Corps and the Legion. The Indians now gave a yell, and fired upon the Grenadier Company, wounding four of them and Lieut.-Col Simcoe. They were driven from the fences, and Lieut.-Col. Tarleton with the Cavalry got among them and pursued them rapidly down Cortlandt's ridge … The Indians fought most gallantly; they pulled more than one of the Cavalry from their horses. (Simcoe 1844: 85–86)

In the end, however, the First Nations warriors were slaughtered, 37 being killed and only two being taken prisoner. The other Americans, a small company commanded by Captain Daniel Williams positioned to the north and west of Mile Square Road, broke after being attacked by the Queen's Rangers, who took eight prisoners.

On September 16, Simcoe targeted the rest of Gist's force, stationed at the bridge across the Saw Mill River. Outflanked on three sides, the Americans, according to *The New-York Gazette and Weekly Mercury* of September 21, "were so briskly charged, that many of them forgot their arms, &c., and fled with the utmost precipitation" west to the Albany Post Road, leaving behind three dead and 35 prisoners. On September 19, a scouting party of Emmerick's men encountered an American patrol of eight men near the little village of Tuckahoe, killing one and capturing the rest. On November 13, Simcoe and Emmerick captured Colonel Thomas Thomas, commander of one of Westchester County's three militia regiments, at his house.

As 1779 dawned, the relentless aggression of the Loyalist companies had advanced a line of control from Yonkers to Eastchester, while the British outpost line ran from Verplanck's Point to the Byram River. McDougall had concentrated all the American regular forces at Peekskill, leaving the county to the east and south defenseless except for the local militia.

Tarleton and Simcoe led successful raids on June 3 and 24. Tarleton led another foray on July 2, routing Colonel Elisha Sheldon's 2nd Continental Light Dragoons and taking eight prisoners and the regimental standard – a victory Tarleton celebrated by despoiling Pound Ridge and Bedford, leaving the churches of both villages in flames.

Patriot Brigadier General Anthony Wayne's victory at Stony Point on July 16 led to a shift in momentum. The Patriots raided Morrisania on August 5, Simcoe's riposte evolving into a running fight through Mamaroneck on August 6. On November 13, Lieutenant Cornelius Oakley, one of the most prominent Westchester Guides, led an attempt to capture DeLancey at his quarters in the Archer House near Kingsbridge, almost under the guns of Fort No. 8. The raid failed in its primary objective, but Oakley returned with five prisoners.

Lieutenant-General Sir Henry Clinton's focus on the South as the primary theater of war led to a de-escalation of the conflict in the North. The British evacuated Newport, Rhode Island, and abandoned 11 of the 12 forts, redoubts, and blockhouses on the Westchester County side of the Harlem

River, leaving only Fort No. 8 garrisoned. On December 26, Clinton, who had succeeded Howe as commander-in-chief of British land forces in North America in February 1778, sailed with Cornwallis for South Carolina, taking Tarleton and Simcoe with him. Lieutenant General Wilhelm von Knyphausen was assigned temporary command of New York operations.

Having returned to take command of the Patriot forces deployed against New York City, Heath found them in a deplorable condition. That winter, New York Harbor froze, cutting off trade and provisioning to the city and putting greater pressure than ever on the requisition of supplies – by whatever means necessary – from Westchester County. In this environment, the raids of DeLancey's Cowboys were endemic.

With the Westchester militia in disarray, the militia from neighboring Connecticut stepped in to take the initiative. Among those active on the border was Captain Samuel Lockwood, who on January 17, 1780, combined his 40 volunteers from Greenwich with another 40 Connecticut militia under Captain Samuel Keeler to target the home in Morrisania of Lieutenant Colonel Isaac Hatfield, commanding officer of the Loyalist Westchester County Militia. As Heath reported to Governor Clinton, Lockwood and Keeler: "… arrived at the place a little after one the next morning, attacked the picket, killed 3 and drove the others in, march'd to the House where Hatfield was, who, with his men took to the chambers [second-floor bedrooms] and kept up a fire down stairs and out at the windows" (quoted in Clinton V.462).

With Hatfield and his men, including Major Thomas Huggerford, Captain Moses Knapp, a quartermaster, and 11 rank and file, having barricaded themselves behind casks of salt and flour, "it appeared difficult, if possible, to dislodge them," Heath commented; accordingly, "the house was instantly set on fire, by putting a straw bed into a closet, which compelled the enemy to jump out at the chamber windows, to avoid the flames" (Heath 1901: 210). The journalist and publisher James Rivington's *The Royal Gazette* reported on January 22 that the house was defended for 15 minutes before the Patriots, having gained possession of the ground floor, set it on fire. After rounding up the Loyalists, the raiders immediately set off back to Connecticut, their prisoners in tow. In the darkness, however, Huggerford somehow slipped away from the column and raised the alarm, mobilizing a rescue party composed of 35 dragoons and 28 infantry, which immediately set off in pursuit.

Leaving the infantry behind at Eastchester under the command of Captain Henry Purdy, Huggerford and his dragoons – a cornet, an adjutant, two sergeants, and 29 privates under the command of Lieutenant Samuel Kipp – raced on ahead. Because the Loyalists in that militia all came from the same communities, they had many ties. Among those captured with Hatfield was his sister Mary's husband, Moses Knapp, while Samuel Kipp was a brother-in-law of another of Hatfield's sisters, Abigail, and he eventually married Mary Knapp, daughter of Moses and Mary, his brother's sister-in-law's daughter.

That strong personal motivation to rescue their friends and relatives notwithstanding, the pursuers were too late to intercept the main body of the Patriot column and liberate those Loyalists taken captive. The rear of the column moved more slowly, however, as Heath reported to Washington: "From what I can learn this would have been a very pretty affair, had not folly & imprudence Stain'd the retreat. The men loitering behind on their return as is commonly the case with this Sort of troops were pursued and overtaken by about 20 Horse who cut and Slashed many of them in a Shocking manner" (Founders Online). The Loyalists ran down the Patriot rearguard between New Rochelle and Mamaroneck, killing 23 of its number and taking another 40 prisoner, some of them wounded (Bell 2020). "We are assured that the only weapon used by Major Huggerford and his determined band of Refugees, in their attack and defeat of Capt. Lockwood's party, was the Sabre," Rivington's *The Royal Gazette* of January 22 noted; "and had not their horses been jaded to a stand-still, every one of the enemy would have fallen into their hands."

From a Patriot perspective, the disappointing denouement to this episode was followed by a complete disaster. On the evening of February 2, a mixed force of British regulars, Hessians, and a company of mounted Loyalists led by Lieutenant Colonel James DeLancey – a total of 500–600 men – set out from Fort Knyphausen under Lieutenant Colonel Chapple Norton. Their target was the 250-man garrison of Continental Army regulars, consisting of five companies drawn from the Massachusetts 1st, 3rd, 9th, 14th, and 15th regiments under the overall command of Lieutenant Colonel Joseph Thompson and stationed at the house of Joseph Young, which had been reoccupied after the British raids two years earlier.

With Norton's contingent taking the Saw Mill River Road, progress for the Crown force was slow. Norton had taken the precaution of fitting out with horse-drawn sleighs, but the snow was so deep even these had to be abandoned, along with the artillery, and despite marching the 20 miles all night on foot the British only reached Young's House at 0900hrs the following morning. Although warned of the enemy's approach, Thompson was determined to stand his ground and fight it out.

It was DeLancey's dragoons who arrived at Young's House first; according to Heath, they "discharged their rifles at long shot, and waited for the coming up of the infantry, where a warm action commenced; the enemy scattered, taking the advantage of the ground and trees in the orchard, and closing up on all sides" (Heath 1901: 213). After 15 minutes under this pressure the Americans broke and either fled or laid down their arms. The British, who burned Young's House to the ground with several wounded Continentals

A Cornishman who entered the British Army as an 18-year-old ensign in 1770, John Graves Simcoe was offered command as lieutenant-colonel of the Loyalist Queen's Rangers in 1777. Like other foreign-born commanders of Loyalist units, such as Lieutenant-Colonel Banastre Tarleton, he proved an aggressive leader, making mobility and surprise his hallmarks in actions around New York City and Philadelphia. His war ended at the battle of Yorktown (1781). Upon returning to England, he was elected to Parliament in 1790 and the following year was appointed Lieutenant Governor of Upper Canada, a post he held until 1798. (Matteo Omied/Alamy Stock Photo)

trapped inside, suffered five dead and 18 wounded. Of these, the Loyalists lost three wounded, Captain Hazard Wilcox mortally. After abandoning 12 prisoners too wounded to keep up en route, the British force returned to Kingsbridge with a haul of 11 Continental Army officers (including Thompson) and 76 rank and file.

In May, Massachusetts troops under Lieutenant Colonel James Millen, who was guided to the Archer House by Westchester Scouts Abraham Dyckman and Cornelius Oakley, captured 34 British soldiers. DeLancey's Cowboys hit back, taking as prisoners a captain and five privates in a raid on Horseneck, Connecticut, on May 5; nine privates at the Byram River on May 10; and 37 in another strike at Horseneck on May 22.

The capture of British Major John André, head of the British Army's Secret Service, on September 23 by three members of the Patriot militia, thereby thwarting General Benedict Arnold's plot to betray West Point and George Washington to the British, was a fillip to Patriot morale. As fall turned to winter and the enlistments of the militia expired, however, conditions in Westchester County went from bad to worse. Lieutenant Colonel John Jameson wrote to Heath on October 18: "The militia and cow boys are very busy driving and it is out of my power to prevent them. If I send the troops down below to prevent the cow boys the militia are busy driving off in the rear and if I have the troops above the lower party, the inhabitants are left destitute without any prospect of redress" (quoted in Sargent 1861: 308).

DeLancey's Cowboys raided at will to the Connecticut line and beyond. On December 9, Huggerford (whose farm in Yorktown had been confiscated and bestowed upon one of André's captors) attacked an American outpost at Horseneck, snaring a lieutenant colonel, a captain, two lieutenants, two ensigns, and upward of 20 rank and file as prisoners. Further raids on December 29 and 31 were repulsed, but the situation was becoming desperate for the Patriots. In a letter dated December 22, Philip Pell, Jr., a member of the State Assembly, labeled Westchester County

> altogether open to the ravages of De Lancey's thieves … Salem [in] the upper part of the County is now the frontier, and it is in the power of De Lancey to destroy that place when he pleases. The People of Westchester County think themselves given up to ruin, are discouraged, and worn out … I believe that unless something is done, Westchester County, in less than a month, will be totally in the Enemy's power. (Quoted in Clinton VI.515)

At this low ebb in Patriot fortunes, Lieutenant Colonel William Hull proposed to wrest back the initiative by striking directly at DeLancey's Cowboys' lair in Morrisania. This was risky, for while the objective, where approximately 450 Loyalists were encamped, was unfortified, it was only 4 miles south of the British stronghold at Kingsbridge and just 2 miles south of Fort No. 8. Washington was skeptical but, given the ongoing strategic stalemate and deteriorating tactical situation, reluctantly approved the plan.

Hull assembled 500 Continentals and 100 volunteer cavalry under Captain Israel Honneywell of the 1st Westchester Militia at Pines Bridge. This force set out on January 21, 1781, with Honneywell's cavalry riding in advance and on the flanks. Leaving three regiments in Eastchester to cover the retreat, the Patriot main force continued its advance via Williams Bridge over the Bronx River, which by prearrangement had been secured by two companies of militia under Captain Dennit and Captain Benton.

Hull then divided his command: 30 men under Captain Daniel Williams were posted to secure DeLancey's Bridge over the Bronx River and then advance on West Farms, while 60 men under Captain Pritchard were detached to cover the Loyalist outpost of 40 men at Throg's Neck. Meanwhile, 100 Continentals under Captain Maxwell were dispatched to cover Fort No. 8 with orders to cut the pontoon bridge linking it to Laurel Hill on the Manhattan side. Hull himself with 400 men would command the assault on Morrisania.

Hull had hoped to launch his attack under cover of darkness, but heavy rain had swollen the normally minor Mill Brook in the path of the American advance to the point where the infantry had to be mounted behind the cavalry in order to effect a ford. This delay meant it was daylight on January 22 when Hull arrived at Morrisania. Nevertheless, the assault was a complete success. The Loyalists, never having anticipated encountering an American raiding party this far south, fled in all directions. After torching the enemy's log cabins, Hull ordered his force to withdraw, having netted 52 prisoners, 60 horses, and the herd of cattle penned at Morrisania.

With the Patriots encumbered by these spoils, progress was slow. Fortunately, Maxwell had been successful in his task of destroying the pontoon bridge, thus forcing the British in Manhattan to take the longer route via Kingsbridge in order to intercept them. Hull and Maxwell linked up with Williams, who was holding DeLancey's Bridge after dispersing the Loyalist garrison stationed in the blockhouse there. The combined force proceeded to the village of Westchester, where, after driving off the Loyalist holdouts sniping at them from the church windows, the Americans broke open the jail, liberating 32 prisoners taken in raids by DeLancey. Pritchard's detachment then rode in, having kept the Loyalists at Throg's Neck pinned down in a drawn-out skirmish. At that point, the entire column commenced its retreat north.

The various American detachments were now pressing hard against the limits of human endurance. Over 24 sleepless hours they had marched, fought, and countermarched more than 40 miles, and now the vengeful British were gaining on them step by step. As Hull approached Eastchester, he formed a rearguard with the 150 men best able to fight, buying time for Maxwell to lead the remainder out of harm's way. Hull was able to hold out until being reinforced when the regiments stationed in Eastchester moved to

The first Governor of the State of New York, George Clinton was elected to the office in June 1777 and served for six successive terms, seven in all (1777–95, 1801–04). He balanced political with military office throughout the war with Britain, being appointed a brigadier general of militia by the New York Provincial Congress in December 1775 and a brigadier general in the Continental Army by Congress in March 1777. He saw action at the battle of White Plains (1776), in the Highlands of the Hudson (1777), and in the Mohawk Valley (1780). Although he subsequently campaigned against ratification of the Constitution, he later served as vice president under Thomas Jefferson and James Madison. (metmuseum.org/ CC0 1.0)

his assistance. Under cover of a winter storm, the Americans were then able to slip away. This raid, the greatest tactical achievement of American arms in this theater of operations to date, cost Hull 12 killed, 13 wounded, and six missing. British losses amounted to 16 killed, 32 wounded, and 52 captured.

The Loyalists were not beaten, however, and Westchester County would not know peace. Throughout that spring, DeLancey mustered his forces for a bold thrust at the strategic crossing of Pines Bridge, which spanned the Croton River. This key chokepoint was guarded by the 1st Rhode Island Regiment, which included many African Americans and Native Americans of the Wampanoag Nation, under the command of Colonel Christopher Greene. A garrison was stationed at the bridge itself while the reserve was stationed further north at Greene's headquarters, Yorktown Presbyterian Church, at the northwest junction of Crompond Road and Old Yorktown Road. Just to the west was Gallows Hill, where one of DeLancey's officers, Lieutenant Edmund Palmer, had been hanged on August 7, 1777 as a spy. By the time Greene arrived, the Crompond Road post had been torched twice by the British.

On May 13, 200 foot and 100 cavalry, led by Lieutenant Colonel James DeLancey in person, departed Morrisania. DeLancey remained in command of the 100 men posted as the covering party on the south bank of the Croton River, while 140 foot and 60 cavalry crossed at the Oblenis Ford 1 mile west of Pines Bridge in the early morning of May 14. Here, taking advantage of scrupulous reconnaissance and intelligence gathering, they were able to exploit a fatal flaw in Greene's dispositions. As Thacher observed, while Greene's sentinels maintained "the greatest vigilance in the night time," he had fallen into the habit of "calling off his guards at sunrise, on the idea that the enemy would not presume to cross in the day time, but the enemy having learnt his mode of performing duty, effected their purpose by crossing the ford immediately after the guard had been withdrawn, and the surprise was so complete that no practicable defence could avail" (Thacher 1827: 255).

The Loyalist raiders then split into two detachments. Captain Moses Knapp, a local who had abandoned his home in the Crompond area early in the war to volunteer with the Lower Party, led 50 men east upriver to take up position in the orchard below the church. Guided by Lieutenant Gilbert Totten, another local, Captain Samuel Kipp, led the main force to the Croton Heights Road, then swung about so as to approach the church from the high elevation northwest of the Richardson Davenport House. The combined Loyalist force swiftly overwhelmed the defenders, killing Major Ebenezer Flagg plus two subalterns and 27 men, and capturing Greene. Their mission accomplished, Knapp and Kipp set out for British lines, taking the direct route via Pines Bridge. Before making much progress Greene, too badly wounded to ride, had to be abandoned at the side of the road, where he died shortly after.

The 30-strong garrison under Ensign Jeremiah Greene guarding Pines Bridge was stationed at the Widow Griffin's House on the north bank. Knapp and Totten rode forward to demand this force surrender. Ensign Greene was prepared to comply and ordered his men to ground their arms, but, according to *The New-York Gazette and Weekly Mercury* of May 21, "After the rebels had, on a summons, consented to surrender, they fired out of the windows of a house into which they had retreated, thereby provoking the conquerors to storm it." Totten having been wounded, after they drove the garrison out

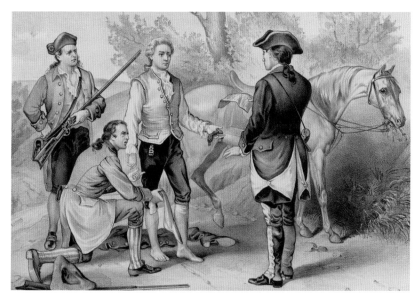

of the house, the vengeful Loyalists pursued the fleeing Americans through the surrounding fields, cutting them down at will. With the bridge secured, the Loyalists continued their retreat south via the Albany Post Road, pausing at the Odell Tavern in Irvington to celebrate before returning to Morrisania.

The arrival of a French expeditionary force in the summer of 1781 shifted the balance of power against the British. On July 22, French dragoons and Connecticut militia drove the Loyalists out of Morrisania and forced them to take refuge on nearby British ships before linking up with the main body of the allied army near Kingsbridge.

Having assessed the state of British defenses, Washington concluded he could neither storm nor besiege New York City. The subsequent departure of the core elements of the American and French armies to the Southern theater of operations opened up Westchester County to renewed outrages at the hands of DeLancey's Loyalists. A petition to Governor Clinton signed by dozens of Westchester County's most prominent citizens importuned him that "we have had a constant & garrisoned Enemy in our County for five years past, who issue out as occasion offers, and destroy and butcher our People" (quoted in Clinton VI.630).

On October 17, DeLancey's Cowboys bagged a party of ten soldiers and eight wagoners with 30 horses, which had been taken south of the Croton for pasture. The action was not one-sided, however. On December 2, a body of 45 of DeLancey's light cavalry under Kipp ambushed a militia officer, Captain Richard Sackett, and two of his men not far from Merritt's Tavern at the upper end of King Street, Harrison. Rather than allow the unit to disintegrate, Sackett's next-in-command, Lieutenant William Mosier, formed his company of 26 men into a solid square with fixed bayonets. In this formation, they stood their ground, repulsing three charges by the Loyalist Cowboys, who were attacking only with swords. The militia held their fire until the Loyalists regrouped for a fourth charge; the first volley of their muskets then killed one man, wounded eight others, and unhorsed two officers, including Kipp, who was trapped beneath his mount and received a bayonet wound severe enough

James Rivington earned notoriety as the most prominent mouthpiece for the Crown in the Americas, but did he play a covert role on the Patriots' behalf? London-born, Rivington emigrated to the colonies in 1760, opened a print shop in New York City, and launched his own newspaper, *Rivington's New-York Gazetteer*, in 1773. His dogged defense of Royal authority led to his being hanged in effigy in April 1775, and the following month a mob of Sons of Liberty attacked his home and printing office, destroying his press and forcing him to flee to a British naval ship in the harbor. After another mob smashed his office and burned his home to the ground in November he sailed for England, only to return to British-occupied New York in 1777 with a new press and an appointment to the £100-per-year role as the king's printer of *Rivington's New York Loyal Gazette*. This publication offered a priceless source of news from a Loyalist perspective. Circumstantial evidence suggests he at some point began working as a double agent for the Culper Ring, the Patriot spy network operating behind British lines in New York City, assigned code number 726 by Benjamin Tallmadge, Washington's head spymaster. (Hulton Archive/Getty Images)

to end his active military career. Thrown into confusion, the Cowboys broke and fled. The initiative and discipline exhibited by Mosier and his company was a significant measure of just how far the militia had evolved over the past five years; men who would have been routed under identical circumstances at the outbreak of the war were now hardened veteran infantry.

There were three more raids into Morrisania during the first three months of 1782 in search of the elusive DeLancey, on January 11, February 26, and finally during the night of March 3/4 when, according to Heath, an American force led by Honneywell "proceeded down between the British fort Number Eight and the cantonment of DeLancey's corps, and having turned the cantonment between daybreak and sunrise, they entered pell-mell. The enemy were completely surprised and fled in every direction" (Heath 1901: 304). The Americans withdrew, taking 21 prisoners with them, and luring the pursuing British retaliatory force into a prepared ambush on the Eastchester Road. Success was total, barring two qualifiers: among the three Americans killed in the raid was the noted Westchester County guide Abraham Dyckman; and while his command was shattered, DeLancey himself remained at large. On April 10 the Loyalists retaliated, raiding as far north as Haverstraw, and forcing Heath to dispatch 200 Continentals to support the Patriot militia.

As negotiations to conclude the war commenced, the informal guerrilla war continued to rage in Westchester County. On January 24, 1783, the Patriots made one last concerted effort to eliminate their nemesis, DeLancey. After mustering at Peekskill, a party of approximately 50 volunteers led by Captain Daniel Williams and Lieutenant John Odell of the Westchester Guides proceeded down the Albany Post Road, turned east at Dobbs Ferry to Tuckahoe, then south via Hunt's Bridge and through Eastchester to West Farms, where DeLancey was residing at his home; but though the Patriots arrived under the cover of total darkness in the early hours of January 25, DeLancey once again eluded capture.

Pursued through Yonkers, the raiding party made a successful stand at Dobbs Ferry and then proceeded to call a halt at the farm of Alfred Orser between Sing Sing and Cortlandt. DeLancey's Cowboys had not abandoned the chase, however; 100 vengeful Loyalists surrounded the farmhouse, leaving the militia, whose horses had been scattered, no option but to make a break for it on foot, some of them being run down while fleeing across the ice of the frozen Hudson River. One of their number was killed in the attempt, and 15 were taken prisoner, among them John Paulding, one of the three captors of Major John André on September 23, 1780. Odell was among those who made good their escape, but only after receiving a saber cut across the bridge of his nose that left a scar he would bear for the rest of his life; and on that ambiguous note, major military operations in Westchester County finally ground to a halt.

On November 25, 1783, the British garrison completed its withdrawal from New York City, and in order to prevent violence, Washington immediately sent in a detachment of the Continental Army. Major General Henry Knox, Washington's trusted artillery commander, led the cheering troops into the city. A little later in the day, Washington and Governor Clinton rode into the city side by side, escorted by a troop of the Westchester Light Dragoons, a Patriot militia unit. This was fitting recognition for the contribution of Westchester County to the Patriot cause.

Oriskany

August 6, 1777

BACKGROUND TO BATTLE

The origins of British grand strategy guiding the 1777 campaign, which culminated in a defeat that constituted one of the critical turning points of the war, can be traced in large part to a fatal misunderstanding concerning the extent of Loyalist sentiment in the former colonies.

The essentials of the operational plan certainly appeared feasible on maps in London. One army under Major-General John Burgoyne would strike south down the Hudson River Valley in New York, while simultaneously a second army under Major-General William Howe would push north from New York City. The two forces would unite at Albany, severing New England from the rest of the fledgling Union. The divided Rebel territories could then be reduced in turn.

This narrative was immediately compromised when Howe instead embarked his army for an amphibious assault on the Patriot capital, Philadelphia. Burgoyne would therefore be on his own, in more ways than one, for the anticipated rising of Loyalists flocking to the Royal Standard on his route of march never happened. On the contrary, he found himself ever more isolated as he drove doggedly on toward Albany, the local Patriot militias responding like antibodies to his invasive presence in their communities, hanging on his flanks, exterminating his outriding forays at Bennington on August 16, and hounding him into surrender at Saratoga on October 17.

For decades prior to the outbreak of war, British authority in the Province of New York had been upheld on the personal recognizance of Sir William Johnson, Superintendent of Indian Affairs for the Northern Colonies. The personal relationship he established maintained peace between the colonists

A patrician of the landed gentry, Major General Philip Schuyler had the difficult task of coordinating the defense of New York against the Burgoyne expedition. When Fort Ticonderoga fell at the onset of that campaign, Schuyler was replaced in command by Major General Horatio Gates, who had accused Schuyler of dereliction of duty. Schuyler demanded a court martial in order to clear his name and was acquitted, but subsequently resigned from the Continental Army. He remained a member of the Second Continental Congress, however, and his high profile made him the target of a British kidnapping plot. Loyalists led by Captain John Meyers broke into Schuyler's mansion, The Pastures, 2 miles south of Albany on July 29, 1781. Schuyler's bodyguards and servants held off the intruders long enough for him to race upstairs and arm himself. As he explained to Washington, "those in the quarter exposed to my fire retired on the first discharge, those that had got in the Saloon, leading to my bed room, retreated with Great precipitation, on hearing me call 'come on my lads surround the house, And Secure the Villains who are plundering'" (Founders Online). Having fallen for this bluff, Meyers' men withdrew, taking with them two prisoners and as much of Schuyler's silverware as they could stuff into their pockets. (Library of Congress)

and the Six Nations of the Iroquois League (*Haudenosaunee*) under the imperial aegis. This responsibility was inherited by his nephew, Guy Johnson, in 1774, while his son, John, inherited his father's baronetcy and lands. These men, along with Sir William's son-in-law, Daniel Claus, the Deputy Secretary of Indian Affairs, struggled to uphold Crown authority before all were impelled to seek refuge in Canada, bringing with them their retainers and many First Nations allies. These regrouped at Fort Ontario and would be employed in the invasion of 1777, but not directly under Burgoyne. Instead, they would form up in a separate column under Lieutenant-Colonel Barry St. Leger. While Burgoyne took the main force directly south, St. Leger's command would be transported west up the St. Lawrence River and via Lake Ontario to use Oswego as its jumping-off point for the march inland. The intent was for this detachment to draw off Patriot forces mobilizing to confront Burgoyne.

St. Leger set out on July 19 with a mixed force including 100-strong detachments from both the 8th and 34th regiments of Foot, 80 Anspach *Jäger*, 40 artillerymen, 200 Canadian pioneers, and approximately 350 Loyalists. At the core of the Loyalist contribution was a unit raised by Lieutenant Colonel Sir John Johnson, the King's Royal Regiment of New York (KRR, unofficially dubbed the Royal Yorkers, Johnson's Greens, or the Royal Greens). Johnson led in person, his key subordinate being his brother-in-law, Captain Stephen Watts. Other prominent Loyalists accompanying the expedition included Colonel Daniel Claus, Superintendent of the Loyalist First Nations in Canada, and Major John Butler, who with his son, Captain Walter Butler, had raised the posse of Loyalist volunteers that would constitute the nucleus of Butler's Rangers when that unit was formally recognized later in the year.

Departing Oswego on July 25, St. Leger linked up with contingents from those four of the six nations making up the Iroquois League that allied with the British – the Mohawk, Seneca, Onondaga, and Cayuga – for this conflict broke the Great Peace (*Kayenarhekowa*) which had bound their confederacy together for generations, sparking a civil war within the greater civil war now raging between rival white factions. The total number of warriors joining the British cause swelled to as many as 1,000 under chiefs such as Thayendanegea (Joseph Brant), Gyantwachia (Cornplanter), Sayenqueraghta (Old Smoke), and Thaonawyuthe (Blacksnake).

The Americans, who had been stretched in holding off a British counter-invasion in 1776 after the Patriot retreat from Montreal, were aware another onslaught out of Canada was inevitable. In March 1777, Major General Philip Schuyler, Patriot commander of the Northern Department, ordered 28-year-old Colonel Peter Gansevoort to take command of the Continental Army's 3rd New York Regiment at Fort Stanwix and make it the breakwater in the defense of the Mohawk Valley. The fort stood on the Oneida Carry, a vital portage road for boats and canoes between the Mohawk River and Wood Creek. The 600 Regulars, laboring to refurbish the fort while coming under ever-increasing pressure from Loyalist and First Nations raiders, were reinforced by another 150 Continental Army troops of the 9th Massachusetts Regiment on July 19. St. Leger arrived beneath the fort with his main force on August 2 and, after Gansevoort refused a summons to surrender the garrison, commenced siege operations. To better impose a tighter cordon,

St. Leger split his command, the British troops encamping north of the fort, the Loyalists and First Nations allies to its south.

With all remaining Regular troops of the Continental Army in the Northern Department being mustered to confront the main British invasion force under Burgoyne, Schuyler would be forced to rely heavily on regional militias to support Gansevoort at Fort Stanwix. This would mean a process of negotiation with, not assumed authority over, military leadership in the local communities. Typically, Schuyler twice ordered Tryon County militia Brigadier General Nicholas Herkimer to reinforce Gansevoort, only for

Thayeadanegea, Joseph Brant the Mohawk Chief.

Joseph Brant (also known as Thayendanegea) was truly a man of two cultures, growing up where the Iroquois and British worlds intersected. As a 12-year-old boy he was a witness to the conference convened at Fort Johnson on June 21, 1755, by Sir William Johnson at which Johnson called on the Iroquois chiefs and clan mothers to ally with the British at the onset of the Seven Years' War. Brant himself would enlist when he came of age, while his sister, Molly, became Johnson's common-law wife. In 1775, Brant withdrew from Patriot authority, first to Canada, then to London with Guy Johnson in order to solicit more direct royal support for First Nations rights. Having been introduced to King George III, he returned to America with the British invasion force that occupied New York City, then made his way north to Six Nations territory, where he raised a company of irregulars dubbed Brant's Volunteers. Interestingly, the majority of these men initially were white Loyalists; only later, as Brant's reputation as a war chief grew, was he able to attract large numbers of warriors from the Iroquois tribes. Brant had numerous opportunities to enhance his credentials in battle, leading from the front at Oriskany (1777); Cobleskill, Wyoming Valley, German Flatts, and Cherry Valley (all 1778); Minisink (1779); Klock's Field (1780); and Lochry's Defeat (1781), among a host of other raids and skirmishes. In the aftermath of the war, he led his people into exile and resettlement in Canada. (Art Images via Getty Images)

Herkimer to insist he could not spare any men. It took a direct appeal from New York Governor George Clinton before Herkimer finally ordered the Tryon County militia mustered at Fort Dayton on August 2. The 800-plus volunteers were organized into four separate regiments, each of about 200 men, and set out on August 4 on the roughly 30-mile trek west to Fort Stanwix. In the vanguard was the Canajoharie District 1st Regiment, under Colonel Ebenezer Cox. Next in line was the Palatine District 2nd Regiment, under Colonel Jacob Klock; then came the Kingston–German Flatts District 4th Regiment under Colonel Isaac Paris and Colonel Peter Bellinger. These were followed by five companies of Colonel Frederick Visscher's Mohawk District 3rd Regiment, then an ox-drawn convoy of 15 wagons bearing provisions and baggage, and finally the rest of Visscher's companies, which were serving as the rearguard.

Herkimer had wanted to wait for reinforcements to come in from the Schenectady and Albany militias, but the local committeemen insisted he march out immediately, even accusing Herkimer of being afraid to advance. In any event, initiative from the neighboring communities would prove lacking. On August 4, Continental Army Colonel Goose Van Schaick wrote to Schuyler from Schenectady complaining that he had ordered half of the militias from Schoharie and Schenectady counties to march immediately to German Flatts only for his orders to be countermanded by the Schoharie committee on the grounds that "none of their Militia can be spared. I have this day been trying to prevail on the militia of this place, but find to my great surprise that not a man will go with me" (quoted in Clinton II.169–70).

Herkimer, meanwhile, was having trouble asserting his authority over his subordinates, who wanted to continue the march along the easier ground north of the Mohawk River. Herkimer had to insist the better option was to cross to the south side at Deerfield in order to avoid risking a river crossing later opposed by St. Leger, even if taking the southern route meant traversing a series of wetlands.

The militia covered a little over 15 miles on August 4. They crossed the Mohawk River at Deerfield the following day and marched on a total of 16 miles to Oriskany, where they camped, 9 miles from Fort Stanwix. Here, Herkimer was very pleased to welcome a war party of some 60–100 Oneidas led by Henry Cornelius Haunnagwasuke and Hanyery Tewahangarahken, the latter accompanied by his wife, Tyonajanegen (Two Kettles Together), along with his son, Cornelius Doxtader, and his brother Honyost. Others with the party included prominent leaders Tonyentagoyan (Blatcop), the brothers Thomas and Henry Spencer, Wakarantharaus (James Powless), and the half-African Kahnawake (Louis Atayataronghta), who would later become famous as Colonel Louis, the highest-ranking Native American in Continental Army service.

That evening, Herkimer dispatched three couriers to Fort Stanwix with news of his impending arrival. Gansevoort was to signal his receipt of the message with three cannon shots, and then sortie to meet the approaching militia column. The couriers had great difficulty slipping undetected through British lines, however, and they did not deliver the message until late the next morning, after that day's battle was already well underway.

As a teenager, Guy Johnson sailed from his native Ireland in 1756 to join his uncle William, Britain's Superintendent of Indian Affairs for the Northern Colonies, in the Mohawk Valley of New York. In 1763, Guy married William's daughter, Mary, and when William died in 1774, Guy succeeded him as superintendent. The advent of war shattered this cozy familial arrangement. In May 1775, Guy fled to Canada; his wife died in Oswego en route. Note how the hybrid cultural nature of Loyalist attachment to the First Nations is emphasized in this painting by the American artist Benjamin West (1738–1820), with Johnson being depicted in a red-coated uniform but with Iroquois moccasins, wampum belt, blanket, and cap. Johnson is accompanied by the Mohawk chief Karonghyontye (Flying Sky), also known to the British as David Hill, to whom they applied the honorific "Captain" for his participation in actions against the Patriots, including the raid on Ballston, Saratoga County (1780). (Heritage Art/Heritage Images via Getty Images)

Animosity flared again between Herkimer, who wanted to wait for the signal from Fort Stanwix, and his senior officers, who demanded an immediate advance, at dawn on August 6. This dispute regarding tactics was exacerbated by preexisting interpersonal tension. While the highly localized nature of militia recruitment would ideally allow for existing communitarian bonds to enhance the collective defense, in some cases preexisting grudges and rivalries would carry through to military service, poisoning the chain of command; and the fact that Herkimer's younger brother, Johannes Yost Herkimer, was serving as a Loyalist captain in St. Leger's army did not enhance his credibility. Having lost control of his command, Herkimer had no choice but to give orders that the entire column stand to arms. In its precipitate enthusiasm, the Patriot militia was walking right into a trap.

MAP KEY

1 *c.*0600hrs: The Loyalists and their First Nations allies take up ambush positions around the road to Fort Stanwix.

2 1000hrs: The Patriot relief column advancing to Fort Stanwix marches into the trap.

3 1015hrs: The ambush is sprung prematurely before the Patriot 1st Regiment reaches the western ravine.

4 1020hrs: In the first minutes of the ambush many Patriot officers are killed or wounded, including the overall commander of the Patriot force, Brigadier General Nicholas Herkimer.

5 1020hrs: First Nations warriors attack the 15 ox-drawn wagons of the Patriot baggage train, trapped on the corduroy road spanning the creek.

6 1020hrs: The Patriot 3rd Regiment is split; those having already cleared the eastern ravine are trapped and cut off, while the rearguard breaks and runs.

7 1030hrs: Led by their Oneida guides, the surviving Patriots of the 1st, 2nd, and 4th regiments regroup north of the road.

8 1030hrs: The remnants of the 3rd Regiment in the rearguard flee to the east.

9 1030hrs: Joseph Brant's volunteers pursue the fleeing Patriots before returning to the main battle site.

10 1050hrs: The Light Company of the KRR attempts to storm the Patriot position, but is repulsed.

11 1100hrs: A summer thunderstorm drenches both sides and forces a hiatus in the action. Herkimer organizes a perimeter based around a pinewood thicket and dispatches a sortie to bring in the remnants of the 3rd Regiment.

12 1105hrs: Lieutenant Colonel Sir John Johnson departs to report on the situation to Lieutenant-Colonel Barry St. Leger encamped opposite Fort Stanwix.

13 1200hrs: Loyalist reinforcements led by the Colonel's Company of the KRR arrive from the British siege lines around Fort Stanwix. Reversing their coats, they attempt to infiltrate the Patriot lines, but the ruse is uncovered and combat erupts.

14 1400hrs: The battle finally winds down when word arrives of a sortie by the garrison of Fort Stanwix. The Loyalists and First Nations warriors break off the engagement and drift away west to salvage what they can from their camps. The Patriots pull back east.

Battlefield environment

Civilization had made little impact on the Mohawk Valley in upstate New York by 1775, but the immense tracts of unspoiled wilderness that defined the region had been contested for generations prior to the outbreak of the American Revolutionary War. The local terrain had been shaped by the rise and retreat of great glaciers during the ice ages, which had carved deep ravines into the bedrock. Much of the surface was covered by a dense deciduous-coniferous forest of hemlock, white pine, beech, birch, and maple. Hunters, traders, settlers, and administrators had long been aware the rivers of the Mohawk Valley provided the only navigable routes connecting the watersheds of the Atlantic Ocean to the Great Lakes, making it a vital crossroads in the networks of commerce and communication spanning the mouth of the St. Lawrence River via Quebec and Montreal to New York City at the mouth of the Hudson River.

The fertile Mohawk Valley in mid-New York State was a critical asset for both sides during the war; and if the British could not retain it, their priority was to deny it to the Patriots. (NYPL/Public Domain)

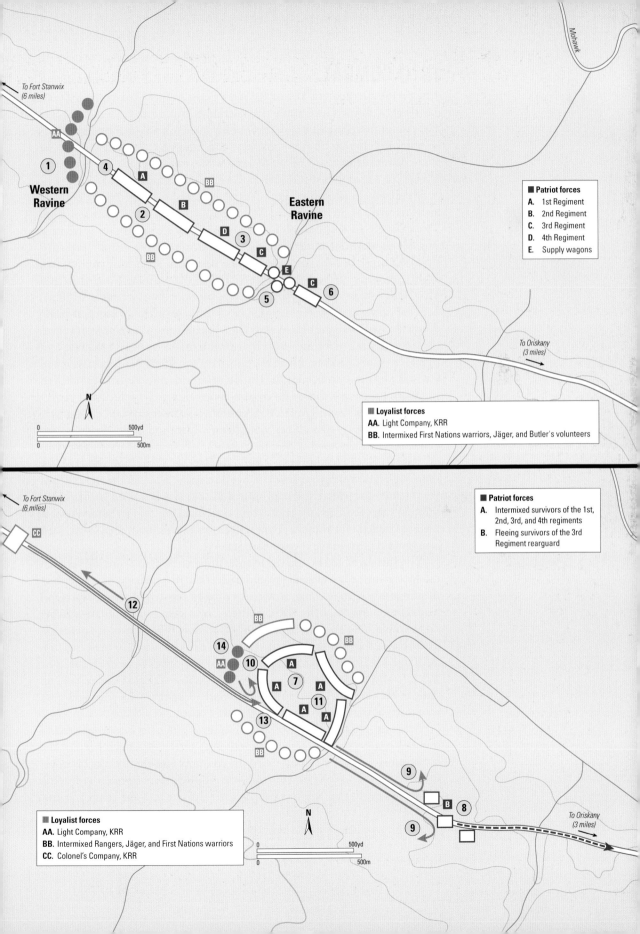

To Fort Stanwix
(6 miles)

AA

① Western Ravine

④

Ⓐ

②

Ⓑ

BB

Ⓓ

③

Ⓒ

BB

Eastern Ravine

Ⓔ

⑤

Ⓒ

⑥

To Oriskany
(3 miles)

Mohawk

■ **Patriot forces**
A. 1st Regiment
B. 2nd Regiment
C. 3rd Regiment
D. 4th Regiment
E. Supply wagons

N

0   500yd
0   500m

■ **Loyalist forces**
AA. Light Company, KRR
BB. Intermixed First Nations warriors, Jäger, and Butler's volunteers

---

To Fort Stanwix
(6 miles)

CC

⑫

BB

BB

⑭

AA

⑩

Ⓐ

⑦

Ⓐ

Ⓐ

⑪

Ⓐ

⑬

Ⓐ

BB

⑨

Ⓑ

⑧

⑨

To Oriskany
(3 miles)

N

0   500yd
0   500m

■ **Patriot forces**
A. Intermixed survivors of the 1st,
2nd, 3rd, and 4th regiments
B. Fleeing survivors of the 3rd
Regiment rearguard

■ **Loyalist forces**
AA. Light Company, KRR
BB. Intermixed Rangers, Jäger, and First Nations warriors
CC. Colonel's Company, KRR

INTO COMBAT

Late on the afternoon of August 5, Joseph Brant had received a message from his sister Molly at Canajoharie that Herkimer was on the march. St. Leger had committed a substantial section of his force to road-clearing operations in order to bring up his heavy artillery, but, informed of this new threat, he immediately determined on a proactive strategy to confront the oncoming Patriot force at as far a distance from Fort Stanwix as possible.

Resolving to keep his line infantry in camp to maintain the siege of Fort Stanwix, St. Leger ordered Major Butler, who had just come in from Three Rivers, to take his volunteers and as many First Nations warriors as possible to block Herkimer's approach. Johnson then successfully prevailed upon St. Leger to take command of the operation, detaching the 55-man Light Company of the KRR under Watts for the purpose. More than 500 First Nations warriors were mobilized. The blocking force set out at 1700hrs, bedding down to camp for the night after a dinner of cold rations, it being deemed unwise to light fires in such close proximity to the enemy's advance.

The site selected for the ambush – about 6 miles east of Fort Stanwix and 3 miles west of Oriskany, where the military road, which ran east to west and was sided by dense woods, passed through two wide ravines that ran north to south – was carefully chosen for maximum advantage. With luck and perfect execution on the Loyalists' part, the Patriots would be trapped on the roadway between the two ravines. They would enter down the slope of the eastern ravine, descending roughly 50ft to its swampy bottom and creek, and cross over the water on a corduroy-log causeway. The road then climbed sharply for some 100ft and swung southwest to bypass a deep ravine on the right. When that feature was passed, the road turned westward and made a gentle climb through mature woods of giant hemlocks. Swinging slightly northward, it then descended into another ravine and crossed a firm-bottomed creek, then rose upward to continue toward Fort Stanwix.

The Patriots would be allowed to enter the stretch of road running between the two ravines. The rearguard would be over the first ravine's corduroy when the vanguard began to climb the western slope of the second ravine. Watts and his Light Company of the KRR, bolstered by a detachment of late-arriving *Jäger*, would hold the western end of the cordon, Watts probably placing a platoon on either side of the roadway, with First Lieutenant George Singleton in charge of one and Second Lieutenant Kenneth McKenzie the other. The warriors of the First Nations and Butler's volunteers pushed east to take up stations on both flanks of the Patriots' route of march, with Joseph Brant's volunteers at the extremities of the Loyalists' lines.

Between 0900hrs and 1000hrs the militia vanguard began its descent into the eastern ravine. Herkimer soon came into view, at the head of the 1st Regiment. These men negotiated the corduroy and climbed the far slope, followed by the 2nd Regiment, then the 4th Regiment, while the leading companies of the 3rd Regiment made their descent into the eastern ravine. Behind them came the trundling ox-drawn wagons.

At this moment of mounting tension, the Loyalist plan went awry, as the ambush was suddenly sprung out of sequence. The intent had been to hold fire until the last militia units had entered the trap; at that moment, the KRR

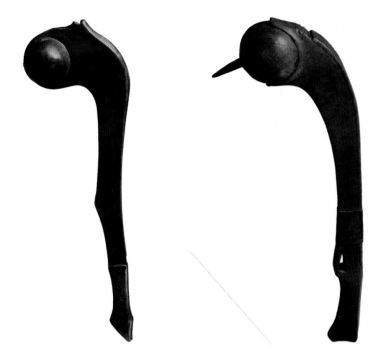

Both elegant and deadly, ball-headed war clubs combine refinement of form with a fearsome efficiency of function. In use for more than 200 years, they were associated with many different First Nations of the Northeast and Great Lakes region. At left is a war club associated with the Anishinaabe culture, Great Lakes region. This weapon was carved as an effigy of a deer's leg. The sculptor carefully chose the hardwood so that the burled portion, where a branch was once attached, would strengthen the angled head. The heavy spherical ball-like weight contained a projecting spike designed to split skulls. Highly polished and decorated with red pigment, this club would have been a warrior's prized possession. The ball of the club on the right is tightly clenched in the jaws of an animal, possibly an otter, and feathers were once tied through the hole above the grip to increase the weapon's supernatural power. (metmuseum.org/CC0 1.0)

would unleash a volley directly into Herkimer's lead companies, the signal for the concealed First Nations warriors to fall upon the enemy's flanks and rear. Instead, through overenthusiasm, miscommunication, or mischance, the first shots rang out somewhere north or south of the road. Within moments, the heights surrounding the Patriot column on three sides were transformed into a sheet of flame as the Loyalists poured fire into their foes' ranks.

Though triggered prematurely, this opening salvo of the ambush was nevertheless devastating. Patriot militiamen the length of the column were shot down in droves. For the survivors, the sensory shock was total. The serene arboreal vistas surrounding them just moments earlier had without warning erupted in violence. All they could see in any direction was gouts of gunpowder smoke. All they could hear was the crash of musketry and the shrill ululation of Iroquois war cries.

Brant's volunteers shattered the 3rd Regiment's leading companies, running down both flanks and keeping up a constant enfilading fire as they proceeded. These warriors moved rapidly through the baggage train which, trapped on the corduroy, erupted into a bedlam of entangled men, animals, and wagons.

The psychological impact of Brant's attack was devastating. Those 3rd Regiment companies at the rear of the column that had not yet entered the eastern ravine simply broke and ran. "The militia in the rear (for the line of march was so scattered as to extend a mile in length) showed but little courage," wrote Continental Army Lieutenant Colonel Marinus Willett, then serving under Gansevoort at Fort Stanwix; "indeed many of them began early to make their escape" (Willett 1831: 52). Writing just three days after the battle, Captain Peter Severinus Deygert, Chairman of the German Flatts Committee of Safety, confirmed: "they took to flight the first firing" (quoted in Clinton II.203). Brant's volunteers pursued them for some time, cutting down many as they fled before circling back to the main action.

Oriskany, August 6, 1777

It is the morning of August 6, 1777, and along the heavily forested trail at Oriskany, New York, battle has erupted. Exposed to an initial volley of fire from three sides simultaneously, the Patriots have already lost scores of men, the bodies of the dead and wounded piling up along the trail. The survivors remain exposed to enemy marksmen; in the foreground, two Loyalists, privates of the Light Company of the King's Royal Regiment, continue to pick out their targets. Meanwhile, First Nations warriors (Mohawk and Seneca of the Iroquois Six Nations) break cover from both sides of the trail to attack at close quarters with war clubs and tomahawks. Patriot resistance is sporadic and on the brink of collapse. Some militiamen loose shots blindly at the puffs of smoke that are all they can see of enemy marksmen sheltering behind the cover of the surrounding wood line.

Bellowing orders to be heard over the din at the other end of the column, Cox labored to form up his vanguard and return fire. When some of the wavering militia attempted to flee he warned he would kill anyone who broke ranks. This was no idle threat; the next man to try it was laid out dead in the road. Cox was himself then shot through the head. Casualties among the Patriot officers were particularly significant for the impact these had on unit cohesion and morale. Within moments of the action commencing, Major John Eisenlord of the Palatine Military District and a secretary to its committee, along with Major Enos Klepsattle of German Flatts, and Major Harmanus Van Slyke, also a native of Palatine, all lay dead. Colonel Samuel Campbell witnessed his nephew, Lieutenant Robert Campbell, being struck by a bullet that killed him instantly.

Herkimer, meanwhile, had spurred back down the column to rally those units following up. As he arrived at Klock's regiment a Loyalist marksman shot down two of the men around him before firing a shot that hit Herkimer's mount, passed through the horse's body, and then through Herkimer's left leg, the soft lead of the musket ball flattening during its passage and, on exiting, shattering the limb in two places. The dying horse collapsed onto the road, pinning Herkimer beneath it. Herkimer was dragged to the relative safety of a low rise on the north side of the road, where he was stretched out under the canopy of a large tree. When his saddle was brought to him he lay propped up against it and continued to issue orders while calmly smoking his pipe and occasionally pointing with its tip to the salient direction in casual emphasis. By thus remaining calm and poised, Herkimer established his authority and began the difficult process of reconstructing effective command and control.

However, it was apparent that before long Herkimer might not have any men left to follow his orders. Caught completely off-guard, strung out on the lower ground between the two ravines, and unable to amass the strength to either push through or regroup to withdraw, the bulk of his command was on the brink of annihilation. Many of the First Nations warriors surrounding the militia were armed not with rifles or muskets but tomahawks and war clubs. Practiced in forest warfare, they would wait until a Patriot had discharged his shot and then dash in to strike at close quarters. Seeking shelter behind whatever cover they could find, the militia learned through bitter experience to work in pairs, the first man firing, then taking a loaded firearm from his partner to shoot any foe attempting to follow up.

Such tactics might work on an individual basis, but as a unit, the Patriot force was disintegrating. Nor was it only the militia taking casualties. The Oneidas who had sided against their erstwhile Mohawk and Seneca brothers in the longhouse of the Six Nations now confronted them face to face and hand to hand. Thomas Spencer and his brother Henry were among the first to fall, but Tonyentagoyan and Louis Atayataronghta continued to rally their warriors. Hanyery Tewahangarahken stood his ground with his wife Tyonajanegen and son Cornelius Doxtader at his side. An article in the September 3, 1777 edition of *The Pennsylvania Journal and Weekly Advertiser* described Hanyery Tewahangarahken as "a friendly Indian, with his wife and son, who distinguished themselves remarkably on the occasion. The Indian killed nine of the enemy, when having receiv[ed] a ball through his wrist that disabled him from using his gun, he then fought with his tomahawk. His son killed two, and his wife on horseback, fought by his side, with pistols during the whole action, which lasted six hours."

Slowly, the Oneida began to move off the road to establish a defensive position along a rise to the north. This rallying point would prove essential to the Patriots' survival for the militia, too, began to re-form on this elevated ground both north and east of the road. Up and down the fragmented militia column, junior officers rallied any men available and formed up in ad hoc defensive positions. Although the brunt of the 3rd Regiment had collapsed, two of its companies, commanded by Captain Jacob Gardinier and Captain John Davis, succeeded in holding the rear of the line. Spotting one of his militiamen being dragged away by a trio of Loyalists, Gardinier succeeded

The confused and close-quarter combat at Oriskany, with the two sides soon intermixed and hundreds of men appearing and disappearing from behind trees and out of musket smoke, was the perfect environment for friendly-fire incidents. (Library of Congress)

Nicholas Herkimer

Born in 1728 to German immigrants, Nicholas Herkimer resided in German Flatts in the Mohawk Valley. He joined the Schenectady Militia and was commissioned a lieutenant in 1758. Elected to head the newly formed Tryon County Committee of Safety in 1775, Herkimer was promoted to brigadier general in the State Militia on September 5, 1776. Reflecting the tangled allegiances that traumatized families throughout the colonies, his younger brother, Johannes Yost Herkimer, declared for the Crown and served under St. Leger's command in 1777; he saw action against the Patriots at Oriskany.

Although Herkimer's preparations were solid, including his attempt to establish contact and joint action with Colonel Peter Gansevoort, he failed to stamp his authority over the militia force, which advanced too precipitously toward Fort Stanwix and walked right into an ambush. Even so, Herkimer's cool and professional leadership once the action began, despite being severely wounded, played a large role in the survival of his shattered command. His wound having become infected, the decision was made to amputate, but the operation went badly and Herkimer died from complications on August 16, 1777.

Brigadier General Nicholas Herkimer effectively lost control of his subordinate officers on the eve of the battle at Oriskany, with the result that his militia walked into an ambush that cost hundreds of lives, including Herkimer himself. The tragedy is that his strategic approach to the relief mission he had been assigned – dispatching messengers to alert the garrison at Fort Stanwix of his approach so the separate Patriot forces could act jointly against the British besiegers – was sound in theory and was playing out in practice when his hand was forced. While his authority as a proactive commander was fatally compromised, however, his qualities as a reactive commander once battle commenced were exemplary. (Smith Collection/ Gado/Getty Images)

in killing all three and returning with the militiaman to this makeshift perimeter.

Colonel Visscher and Colonel Volkert Veeder, meanwhile, strove to re-form the regiment as a unit. Visscher struggled back along the column toward the corduroy, threatening to shoot anyone who ran, rallying his men, and driving them forward with his sword to link up with the 4th Regiment. In the midst of his exhortations a musket ball passed so close to his head that his queue was severed and a bloody welt raised on his neck.

Simultaneously, Bellinger's companies, under a punishing fire from both flanks, advanced to join Klock's men. With clubbed muskets and bare hands, the combined 2nd and 4th regiments drove the Loyalists from the edge of the higher ground to the north of the road and then formed into a defensive circle, onto which the 1st Regiment fell back. At this point, about 45 minutes after the ambush commenced, the action settled into an exchange of fire between the Loyalists and the now fully enclosed Patriots.

In order to break up this intensifying militia resistance, Johnson resolved to commit his KRR in a frontal assault. Advancing in two ranks led by Watts, Singleton, and McKenzie, the Loyalist unit unleashed a volley as it closed with the 1st Regiment before charging into the Patriot ranks, a defiant Highland roar echoing through the trees – but a single light company lacked the momentum necessary to storm even a hastily prepared defensive line. Firing from under cover, the Patriots halted and then drove back the KRR charge.

The standoff continued until around 1100hrs, when a sudden summer downpour forced the combatants on both sides to cease fighting immediately and take whatever shelter they could in order to keep their powder dry. While the thunderstorm raged, Johnson left Watts and Butler in command and departed for the British encampment in order to provide St. Leger with a situation report, intending to return with sufficient reinforcements to finish the off the beleaguered Patriots.

On his side, Herkimer took this opportunity to reorganize the surviving militia of his command, now reduced to approximately 40 percent of its original strength. The remnant of the Patriot force retreated to the relative security of a pinewood thicket, a natural redoubt studded with fallen trees that offered the defenders the advantage of cover. This position occupied the

Sir John Johnson

When Sir William Johnson died in 1774 his son John inherited the family's lands in frontier New York, his father's long-established relationship with the Six Nations, and a noble title via a knighthood bestowed by King George III. Warned that Major General Sir John Johnson was mustering his First Nations allies and Loyalist tenants, in January 1776 General George Washington dispatched a force to neutralize this threat; Johnson broke his parole in May and fled to Canada.

Lieutenant Colonel Sir John Johnson raised the Loyalist King's Royal Regiment of New York and served under St. Leger in 1777. At the climax of a destructive raid into the Schoharie and Mohawk valleys, on October 19, 1780, Sir John (who had earned the Iroquois name Owassighsishon, or He Who Makes The Roof To Tremble) and his mixed force routed a 380-strong Massachusetts Militia detachment under Colonel John Brown at Stone Arabia in the Palatine District. Sir John was promoted to brigadier general in 1782 and also appointed as Superintendent General and Inspector General of Indian Affairs in Canada, a post he held until his death on January 4, 1830.

---

space between the first ravine to the east and the second ravine to the west, while holding the high ground on its northern flank, where the slope fell off to a bog, beyond which was the river. In order to dislodge their foe, from almost every angle, except for the narrow open road, the Loyalists would have to attack upslope. While the Patriots tightened their lines, Herkimer dispatched Bellinger to retrieve the three isolated companies of Visscher's men remaining on the lower ground. This sortie succeeded in retrieving the remnants of the 3rd Regiment, thereby consolidating the militia's manpower within a single defensive perimeter.

Johnson, meanwhile, had succeeded in reporting to St. Leger, who ordered the Colonel's Company of the KRR and whatever other detachments were available to march out for the ambush site under Captain-Lieutenant Donald John McDonell. When these reinforcements arrived, Butler devised a ploy by which to infiltrate the enemy's position. In order to create the impression they were reinforcements arriving from Fort Stanwix, the men of the Colonel's Company were ordered to reverse their coats and proceed with drums beating into the Patriot lines. At first, this ruse was successful; one Patriot militiaman, seeing an acquaintance among the oncoming file, exultantly broke ranks to greet him. The subterfuge collapsed, however, when the baffled militiaman was seized by his extended hand and hauled into the KRR line as a prisoner.

Butting and thrusting with his spontoon, Gardinier, a blacksmith by trade, ran forward to recover his captive militiaman. McDonell and two of his Royal Greens grappled with Gardinier, forcing him to the floor and pinning him to the ground with a bayonet thrust through each thigh. McDonell attempted to finish him off with a bayonet to the chest, but Gardinier took the blade in his bare hand and, as McDonell lunged forward, seized him in a bear hug, using his body as a shield. A militia private, Adam Miller, rushed to the rescue, felling one of the Loyalists who was bayoneting Gardinier. McDonell wrenched himself free of Gardinier in order to attack Miller, but Gardinier in turn thrust the tip of his spontoon up into McDonell's throat, killing him instantly.

The rest of the militia, still unaware the Colonel's Company was a Loyalist unit in disguise, were horrified at this spectacle. "For God's sake, Captain," some shouted, "you are killing your own men!" "They are not our men!" Gardinier roared back; "They are the enemy – fire away!" (quoted in Bunce 1870: 267).

Sir John Johnson was the only son of Sir William Johnson and his common-law wife, Catherine Weissenberg. He inherited his father's lands and titles, but had to earn the respect among the Iroquois his father had built up over decades. The war intervened almost immediately, and although Sir John's loyalism cost him his family's inheritance at Johnson Hall, it enabled him to build a reputation as a warrior prepared to fight alongside the First Nations on the field of battle and represent their interests at the council table. He continued to fulfill the latter role right up until his death more than four decades after the war's conclusion. (Wikimedia/Public Domain)

The Patriots unleashed a volley, but the Colonel's Company, close enough now to have compromised the outer ring of the Patriot defensive perimeter, charged and broke the militia line. Desperate close-quarter fighting then erupted.

In a representative episode, three Loyalists of the Colonel's Company sought to kill or capture Captain Andrew Dillenbeck. An officer in the Palatine Military District, Dillenbeck was the son of German immigrants who had settled in the Mohawk Valley and were still residing there. Fluent in English, German, French, and Iroquois, he was a frontier intellectual well-versed in the fate of prisoners and who had accordingly vowed he would never be taken alive. When the first Loyalist seized Dillenbeck's musket in a bid to wrest in out of his hands, Dillenbeck responded by smashing the weapon's stock into his opponent's face. He then shot the second Loyalist and thrust his spontoon into the body of the third. This rampage was brought to an abrupt end when Dillenbeck was struck by an incoming round that killed him instantly. Family tradition maintained the shot that killed him was fired by a Loyalist who had lived on the farm adjoining the Dillenbeck homestead. The two men were related by marriage; just one of the countless fratricidal casualties of this conflict that pitilessly pitted neighbor against neighbor.

Both sides finally disengaged when the balance suddenly tipped dramatically in favor of the Patriots. It was only when the couriers dispatched by Herkimer the previous day finally arrived at Fort Stanwix late in the morning that Gansevoort became aware militia reinforcements were incoming. He immediately ordered a sortie under Willett, but this was delayed by the same thunderstorm that forced a hiatus in the fighting along the trail. When the skies cleared, Willett succeeded in storming and plundering the Loyalist and First Nations encampments south of the fort, which had been left for all intents and purposes unguarded by the commitment of virtually their entire strength to the ambush. So much loot was accumulated Willett had to send for wagons to haul it back into the fort. This he accomplished before St. Leger could intercept him with the regular British troops under his command.

The shocking news that their camp was being plundered induced the Iroquois warriors at the ambush site, already disheartened by their heavy casualties, especially the loss of so many war captains, to melt away from the still-raging battle in a bid to salvage what they could. Bereft of their allies, the Loyalists of the KRR and Butler's volunteers had no choice but to withdraw, and with them the *Jäger*. So precipitate was this disengagement that many wounded were abandoned, among them Watts, left behind with his leg torn open and a punctured throat. The survival of Herkimer's command therefore hinged on his decision to forward the couriers to Gansevoort and their arrival at the fort. According to one surviving Patriot, Hugh McMaster of the 3rd Regiment, the destruction of the entire militia was prevented only by the intervention of the sortie.

The aftermath was ugly. As Major Butler wrote to Lieutenant-General Sir Guy Carleton on August 15, many of the militia prisoners taken in the battle were afterward killed. This reflected the vengeful mood of the First Nations. Their warriors had constituted the bulk of the Loyalist force, had during the battle displayed what Butler considered the greatest zeal for the royal cause, and "had they not been a little too precipitate, scarcely a Rebel of the party" would have escaped; "Most of the leading Rebels are cut off in the action so

that any further attempt from that quarter is not to be expected" (quoted in Stone 1851: 243). The cost, however, had been steep, the First Nations suffering 33 warriors killed and 29 wounded.

Fought in the complete absence of British or Patriot regular troops, the battle of Oriskany was in terms of percentages of killed and wounded the bloodiest battle of the American Revolutionary War. Roughly one-quarter of the Loyalists involved in the ambush were killed or wounded, among them Watts, who through sheer force of will survived two forsaken days alone on the battlefield before being brought in by Iroquois scouts. His wounded leg was too badly damaged to be saved, but he otherwise recovered.

The Patriots lost approximately 40 percent of their number killed in action. Including the wounded and those taken prisoner (many of whom were subsequently tortured to death), total casualties among the militia represented a staggering 60 percent. The heart of an entire community's manhood had been effectively cut out; more than half of the officers were killed or wounded, including most of the Committee of Safety members. Among them was Herkimer: he survived the battle, but not the subsequent amputation of his left leg, dying on August 16. St. Leger could with justification write to Burgoyne on August 11 that "The completest victory was obtained. About four hundred lay dead on the field, among the number of whom were almost all the principal movers of rebellion in that country" (quoted in Stone 1851: 241).

St. Leger failed to follow up on his advantage, however. On August 7, Sayenqueraghta (whose son, Tocenando, had fallen in battle the previous day) and Brant approached Johnson and Claus with a proposal to consummate the victory at Oriskany by raiding into the now defenseless Tryon County. St. Leger declined, on the grounds there were insufficient troops to prosecute the siege while also pursuing independent action. A more aggressive policy may have paid off, for as Claus later wrote of the Mohawk Valley, "The inhabitants in general were ready (as we afterward learned) to submit and come in" (quoted in Beach 1879: 144).

There is evidence that zeal for the Patriot cause in New York was flagging. Deygert, Herkimer's brother-in-law, wrote Schuyler from Canajoharie on August 6 with the grim news that on the march to Fort Stanwix "the Militia were attacked and according to what information I have as yet received, the Militia are entirely cut to pieces; the General is killed with most of the Field Officers" (quoted in Clinton II.191). Deygert begged Schuyler to "immediately send assistance or this quarter must of course fall into the enemies hands, as the whole of the Militia was in the engagement except a few guards consisting of old men and those not able to march. So we cannot if the accounts received be true (which there is too much common ground for) raise another force to make any stand with" (quoted in Clinton II.191–92).

"The flower of our Militia either killed or wounded," Deygert wrote in desperation to his counterparts in Albany on August 9; "Gentlemen, we pray you will send us succours [sic]. By the death of the most part of our Committee members, the Field Officers and several being wounded, every thing is out of order, our people entirely dispirited ... we cannot hope to stand it any longer without your aid" (quoted in Clinton II.203–04). The Albany Committee of Safety had little to offer the war effort beyond defeatist prognostications, informing the State Council at Kingston on August 11 that "The appearance of a few of the enemy's troops on the Mohawk River would immediately make the inhabitants lay down their arms" (quoted in Clinton II.209). Although the feared British incursion did not come, the Tryon County militia was shattered and never fully recovered. Governor Clinton was forced to intervene and amalgamate the available manpower in Tryon County with that of Albany County, an arrangement that continued until 1781.

Meanwhile, the siege of Fort Stanwix intensified. St. Leger's guns had been brought up and commenced a steady drumbeat of fire, while the Loyalists slowly drove trenches toward the walls. The British 6-pounders proved too light to impact the defenses, however. Spirits rose briefly on August 15, when more than 100 Loyalist volunteers arrived from Schoharie County, where they had just fought a skirmish with Continental Army Light Dragoons at the Flockey. Such was the despondency in the siege lines, however, that many of these men immediately opted to return home.

Patriot morale, conversely, remained high. Gansevoort steadfastly refused to countenance surrender, while Willett succeeded in slipping through British lines and reporting to Major General Benedict Arnold, who was marching

up from Albany with a relief force composed of the 1st and 4th New York regiments of the Continental Army. Given the suffering of the communities through which he was advancing, Arnold could not look for reinforcement from their decimated militias; his most earnest entreaties notwithstanding, fewer than 100 men rallied to his colors (Watt 2011: 243).

For St. Leger, time was running out. A party he had sent to recruit for the Loyalist cause in the Mohawk Valley, led by Captain Butler, had not only failed to bring in volunteers, but also its members had been arrested and sentenced to death for treason; Butler himself succeeded in escaping and fleeing to Canada. His First Nations allies, still mourning their lost brothers and dispirited by the plundering of their camp, were growing more frustrated by the day over the drawn-out siege. The news that Arnold was advancing proved to be the last straw, as the outnumbered and makeshift British coalition could not hope to stand its ground against another Continental Army force closing on its rear while one already lay at its front. With the Iroquois already melting away, St. Leger had no option but to order a general retreat on August 22. This quickly degenerated into a rout, however, sparked by a false rumor that the Patriot relief force was already astride the return route to Canada. Abandoning their guns, wagons, and stores, the British took to their boats and fled back the way they had come.

The site of the ambush at Oriskany, meanwhile, slowly returned, undisturbed, to nature, human bones being observed scattered through the woods years later. The Loyalist victory ultimately availed them nothing, however. Having repelled St. Leger and neutralized this threat to his left flank, Arnold took charge at Saratoga and led his men to a famous, and decisive, victory two months later.

Kings Mountain

October 7, 1780

BACKGROUND TO BATTLE

Lieutenant-General Sir Henry Clinton did not call on the Loyalists for aid when his army landed in South Carolina on February 12, 1780, as he did not want them to rise prematurely. It was only when Patriot authority in South Carolina completely collapsed upon the surrender of Charleston on May 12 that he felt empowered to cultivate local support. On May 22, Clinton assigned responsibility for rallying the Loyalists to Major Patrick Ferguson, who was named Inspector General of Militia. Ferguson, who had lost the use of his right arm during the battle of Brandywine on September 11, 1777, understood his role required him to balance discipline with tact. As a consequence, the men of each new company raised were allowed to elect their own commanding officer, and were given assurances they would not be required to serve outside Georgia or the Carolinas.

Discouraged Patriots, meanwhile, trooped in, among them prominent officers like Major Andrew Pickens and Major Andrew Williamson, to accept the terms of surrender and return home. Clinton, however, overplayed his hand when, shortly before departing for New York, leaving Lieutenant-General Charles, Lord Cornwallis in command, he issued a proclamation warning any who failed to swear allegiance to the Crown would be considered rebels and treated accordingly. This left no room for neutrality. Even those Patriots who had accepted paroles in good faith were driven back into the field by British intransigence, and the embers of civil strife swiftly burst into flame again.

Cornwallis distributed his forces throughout South Carolina, keeping Lieutenant-Colonel Banastre Tarleton and the prowling dragoons of his British Legion in reserve while stationing Lieutenant Colonel Thomas

Brown and his Florida Rangers at Augusta, Georgia; Colonel Nisbet Balfour with three regiments of the Loyalist Provincial Corps at Ninety Six, South Carolina; Lord Rawdon with his Volunteers of Ireland and two regiments of regulars at Camden, South Carolina; and Colonel George Turnbull with a regiment of DeLancey's Brigade at Rocky Mount, North Carolina. The intent was to use these strongholds as rallying points for local Loyalist volunteers who would, it was hoped, come flocking to the colors.

On May 29, Tarleton's British Legion annihilated a Continental Army force at the Waxhaws, near Lancaster, South Carolina. However, this victory served more to inflame Patriot spirits than cow them. On the same day, Colonel William Bratton scattered Loyalist militia at Mobley's Meeting House near Winnsboro, South Carolina. Cornwallis did not want the Loyalists to rise in North Carolina until he could arrive there to support them; but King George III's Loyalist allies continued mustering, the total congregating at Ramseur's Mill rising to 1,300. Had this force succeeded in linking up with Cornwallis, British authority would have been substantively reinforced. As Cornwallis had feared, however, Patriot militia Colonel Francis Locke of Rowan County at the head of just 400 men surprised and scattered the Loyalists on June 20.

Over a four-day period in mid-July, Loyalist and Patriot partisans clashed at Union Court House, Williamson's Plantation, Cedar Springs, Gowen's Old Fort, and McDowell's Camp on the Pacolet River. The defeat of Christian Huck, a captain in Tarleton's British Legion, by militia Colonel William Bratton at Williamson's Plantation on July 12 was particularly decisive, in that it showed the militia could stand up to the dreaded Loyalist dragoons. Huck and 35 of his officers and men were killed outright, 50 were wounded, and a dozen of the rest were captured. The Americans lost just one killed and one wounded. At the end of July, 600 Patriot militia, including the Overmountain men of North Carolina under Colonel Isaac Shelby, bluffed the entire 93-man Loyalist garrison at Thicketty Fort into surrendering, by some accounts after rigging a dummy field gun out of a log.

Another Patriot militia force under Brigadier General Thomas Sumter targeted Hanging Rock, the most northerly of the British strongholds, guarding the Camden–Charlotte road. This position was stoutly garrisoned with more than 1,400 British troops, including the 500-man Prince of Wales' Royal American Volunteers, local Loyalist militia, and 160 infantry detached from Tarleton's British Legion. On August 1, Major William Davie, the 24-year-old commander of a company of North Carolina militia dragoons, ambushed and destroyed three companies of North Carolina Loyalist militia, taking no prisoners. A general action on August 6 resulted in another British defeat when the Patriot militia successfully stormed Hanging Rock, but they were unable to follow up this advantage because the men fell to looting the enemy's camp, discovering stores of rum in the process. Sumter was reluctantly obliged to withdraw, having inflicted 200 casualties for the loss of 12 killed and 41 wounded.

Cornwallis assumed his smashing defeat of the Continental Army at Camden on August 16 would crack the resolve of the Patriot resistance. The British ascendancy appeared complete just two days later when Sumter, withdrawing toward North Carolina with prisoners and 80 seized British supply wagons, was surprised at Fishing Creek by Tarleton's dragoons.

Lieutenant-Colonel Banastre Tarleton is depicted in this 1782 portrait by the British artist Sir Joshua Reynolds (1723–92). The mixed respect and loathing with which Tarleton was held in Patriot circles is beautifully illustrated by the reference to him as "That enterprising, though inhuman young officer" in *The New-Jersey Gazette* on February 21, 1781. In 1773, at the age of 19, Tarleton inherited £5,000 on the death of his father. Having otherwise squandered this inheritance, in 1775 he purchased a commission as a cornet in the 1st Dragoon Guards, and sailed for America. He scored his first coup in 1776, when he captured Continental Army Major General Charles Lee in Basking Ridge, New Jersey. Rising rapidly through the ranks, Tarleton subsequently saw action in the Pennsylvania campaign (1777–78) and in Westchester County, New York, before sailing for the South, where his reputation as the Patriot *bête noire* was truly established at such clashes as Waxhaws (1780), Fishing Creek (1780), and a host of other anti-partisan operations. After nearly capturing Virginia Governor Thomas Jefferson in a raid on Monticello in 1781, he was caught up in the British surrender at Yorktown later that year. (Universal History Archive/Universal Images Group via Getty Images)

Though the British Legion was outnumbered by more than four to one, "it was a perfect rout, and an indiscriminate slaughter," James Collins recalled; "No quarter was given" (Collins 1859: 42). The Patriots lost more than 150 men killed or wounded and 300 captured. Sumter himself barely escaped, while Tarleton's men were able to liberate the prisoners of war and the entire purloined supply train, including artillery, small arms, and 800 horses.

Nevertheless, the Patriots fought on. Militia Colonel Elijah Clarke and Shelby had spent the summer on the run from Ferguson, his advance units clashing with them at Cedar Springs on August 8 before they slipped away. On August 19, Clarke and Shelby led a raid on the combined British and Loyalist garrison guarding a ford of the Enoree River at Musgrove Mill, using a detached force to draw the British garrison out of its prepared position and into an ambush. The Crown lost 63 killed, 90 wounded, and 70 captured; the Patriots only four killed and 12 wounded. Fighting his own guerrilla war, Lieutenant Colonel Francis Marion scored his first victories on September 4, 1780, defeating Loyalist militia in two separate engagements at Britton's Neck and Blue Savannah, and smashed another Loyalist militia at Black Mingo Creek on September 30.

Cornwallis, meanwhile, had advanced to Charlotte, North Carolina. His left (western) flank was shielded by Ferguson, who marched west hoping to raise and organize Loyalist volunteers from the backcountry. He raided Gilbert Town on September 7, and scored a minor victory over Colonel Charles McDowell at Cane Creek on September 12, forcing the militia to withdraw to the far side of the Blue Ridge Mountains. Fatally, Ferguson dispatched a messenger to warn the population that "If they did not desist from their opposition to the British arms, he would march over the mountains, hang their leaders, and lay their country waste with fire and sword" (Draper 1881: 169). This was a bluff, however, and far from intimidating the communities residing along the frontier, it spurred something akin to a total mobilization.

The militias were summoned to muster on September 25 at Sycamore Shoals, Tennessee, where 160 men under McDowell had encamped after being driven west by Ferguson. On the appointed day, Shelby rode in from the Holston River valley with 240 men, Lieutenant Colonel John Sevier

The battle of Waxhaws on May 29, 1780, established Tarleton's reputation as the most formidably aggressive officer in the British ranks, but also as a hated foil for the Patriot cause. A single charge by Tarleton's mounted Loyalist British Legion and 17th Light Dragoons easily overwhelmed Colonel Abraham Buford's mixed force of Regulars and militia, but, leading from the front, Tarleton himself had his horse shot out from under him. In his memoirs, he admits "slaughter was commenced" before he could regain control of his men, which he ascribed to "a report among the cavalry, that they had lost their commanding officer, which stimulated the soldiers to a vindictive asperity not easily restrained" (Tarleton 1787: 31–32). Surviving Patriots maintained most of their compatriots were massacred in cold blood after surrendering, and the motto "Tarleton's Quarter!" became a Patriot rallying cry. (Smith Collection/Gado/Getty Images)

brought 240 more from communities along the Nolachucky River, and Colonel William Campbell contributed 200 men from just over the line in Virginia, another 200 arriving from that quarter independently.

This assembly reflected the extent to which the backbone of the Patriot war effort was the dedication of entire families to its cause. Sevier was accompanied by two of his sons – Joseph, the oldest at 18, and James, who was almost 16 – and two of his brothers, Captain Valentine Sevier and Captain Robert Sevier. Shelby, unmarried, had no sons, but his two brothers also had rank with the militia, namely Major Evan Shelby, Jr., and Captain Moses Shelby. A relative by marriage of Sevier's first wife was John Crockett, the father of the legendary Davy Crockett, and John brought three more members of the Crockett family with him. No fewer than 12 Campbells from Washington County, Virginia, were in the force, all of them in one way or another related to their commanding officer.

The Overmountain men set out the next day, Tuesday, September 26, crossing the Blue Ridge Mountains to rendezvous at Quaker Meadows with Colonel Benjamin Cleveland at the head of 350 more militia. By September 30, nearly 1,300 men were on the headwaters of the Catawba River. By consensus, Campbell was nominally in command, but the actual rules of engagement were laid down by Shelby: "When we encounter the enemy, don't wait for the word of command. Let each one of you be your own officer and do the best you can. If in the woods, shelter yourself and give them Indian play" (quoted in Draper 1881: 196).

Ferguson, concerned about his exposed position, had withdrawn to Gilbert Town, where he received the first reports of the Patriot force moving against him. He broke camp and marched east, seeking to link up with Cornwallis at Charlotte. The Overmountain men, convinced he was marching south for Ninety Six, lost his trail. It was only on October 6, when they reached Cowpens, South Carolina, and linked up with more militia that they received intelligence of Ferguson's intentions. A council of war resolved to make a forced march to overtake the Loyalists before they could make good their escape. For this purpose, 910 men were chosen, taken largely from those regiments that had the freshest mounts. At 2100hrs this force began to push rapidly eastward, traveling all that night and the next day through heavy rain.

Ferguson, meanwhile, had elected to halt on the evening of October 6 and make camp at Kings Mountain, a steep hill that rises abruptly 800ft above the low hills of the Carolina piedmont. Its mesa-like crest was relatively clear and ran from northeast to southwest for about 500yd. At the narrow southwest end it was 60–70yd across, widening to nearly 200yd at the northward end, where Ferguson's men and wagons were drawn up. Though he was only a day's march from Charlotte, he elected not to break camp the following morning, and though he could have made his position even more secure by erecting abatis, breastworks, and redoubts from the abundant stones and logs available, he neglected to do so. He dispatched a courier to Cornwallis requesting reinforcements, but was too late in doing so. That same day, Sevier's scouts captured some outriding Loyalists who, under interrogation, revealed Ferguson's position and the locations of his pickets. By the afternoon of Saturday, October 7, the Patriots had closed up to Kings Mountain.

Rising from captain at the beginning of the war to brigadier general by its end, the tactical acumen and leadership qualities of Francis Marion single him out as perhaps the greatest exponent of guerrilla warfare in the history of North America. After the twin disasters at Charleston and Camden in 1780, Marion's command of a few dozen irregulars was effectively the sole fighting force still in arms for the Patriot cause in South Carolina at the end of that summer. So effective was he in rising to this challenge a frustrated Lord Cornwallis wrote to Lieutenant-General Sir Henry Clinton complaining that "there was scarcely an inhabitant between the Santee and Pedee, that was not in arms against us" (quoted in Simms 1846: 141). Marion always sought reconciliation with his foes and never allowed personal considerations to cloud his judgment. He scrupulously upheld the conventions of war even after Loyalists captured his 16-year-old nephew, Gabriel Marion, and executed him upon learning of his relationship to the legendary "Swamp Fox." (NYPL/Public Domain)

1 Morning, October 7: Although ostensibly retreating east to link up with the main British army under Lieutenant-General Charles, Lord Cornwallis, Major Patrick Ferguson elects to remain encamped with his Loyalist force atop Kings Mountain. Aware a Patriot force is pursuing him, he dispatches messengers to Cornwallis requesting reinforcements, but although having decided to stand and fight, neglects to fortify his position.

2 c.1400hrs: Having concentrated west of the Loyalist position, the Patriot rank and file tie off their horses and, led by their still-mounted officers, march out in their regiments to encircle Kings Mountain. Because of the variable terrain and distances involved the Patriot regiments close up to Kings Mountain unevenly.

3 1500hrs: The first shots are exchanged.

4 1505hrs: Ferguson orders his Provincials to lead a bayonet charge that drives Colonel William Campbell's men back down the south side of the slope.

5 1510hrs: Ferguson withdraws the Provincials, re-forms them at the summit, and sends them charging down the hill's north face against Colonel Isaac Shelby's men.

6 1510hrs: Ten minutes after the action commences at the western end of Kings Mountain, the last Patriot regiments finally close the circle at the eastern end of the line, cutting off Ferguson's last chance to escape.

7 1520hrs: The Provincials stabilize the Loyalist position at the eastern end of the line.

8 1535hrs: After a seesaw struggle of charge and countercharge, the critical turning point is reached at the western end of Kings Mountain when the redeployment of the Provincials is interpreted by the Loyalist militias, already running low on ammunition, as a retreat. The Loyalists begin to abandon their positions amid an escalating rout.

9 1540hrs: As the Loyalist position collapses, the Patriots claim the heights on the western edge of Kings Mountain and begin pushing east along the ridge.

10 1545hrs: The Patriots begin to close up to the Loyalists from all sides.

11 1550hrs: Ferguson attempts to break out on horseback, but is shot out of his saddle.

12 1555hrs: A last charge by the Provincials along the ridge is repulsed.

13 1600hrs: Surrounded and hemmed in, the Loyalists surrender. The battle is over.

Battlefield environment

Kings Mountain is located in the Piedmont Region of the Carolinas, a transition zone between the coastal plain to the east rising up into the Blue Ridge Mountains to the west. Gently rolling hills with many stream-cut valleys characterize the region. The landscape in 1780 was dominated by oak, hickory, and pine forest. The first European settlers were subsistence farmers; cotton would not come to define the region until a later generation.

Kings Mountain today. South Carolina Loyalist militia officer Colonel Robert Gray was critical of Major Patrick Ferguson's decision to make a stand here for, "although he knew his danger" and was withdrawing to link up with Lord Cornwallis, "he loitered away two days most unaccountably at Kings Mountain," giving time for the Patriot militias to close up to him (Gray 1910: 142). (Zachary Frank/Alamy Stock Photo)

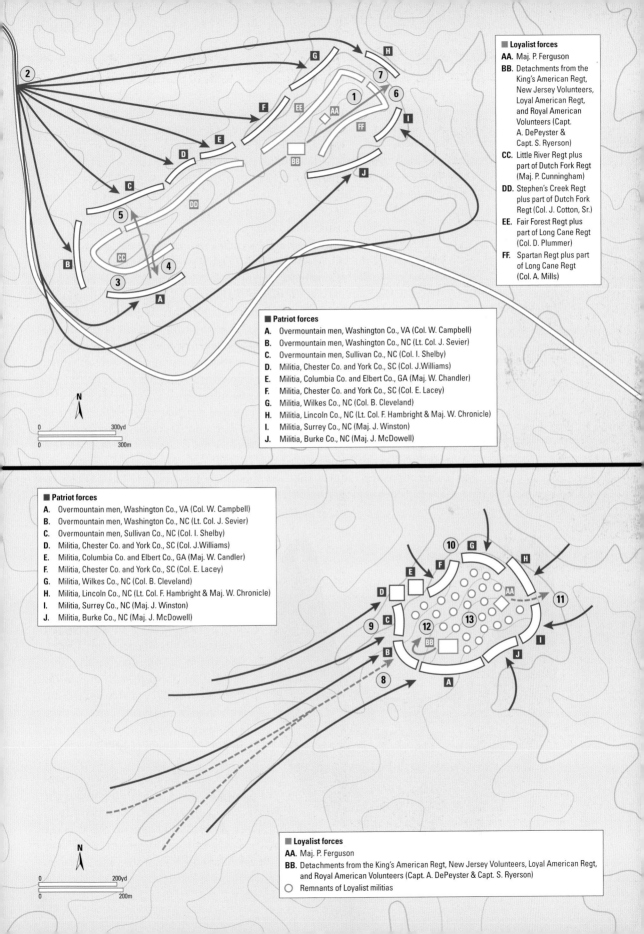

Loyalist forces

AA. Maj. P. Ferguson

BB. Detachments from the King's American Regt, New Jersey Volunteers, Loyal American Regt, and Royal American Volunteers (Capt. A. DePeyster & Capt. S. Ryerson)

CC. Little River Regt plus part of Dutch Fork Regt (Maj. P. Cunningham)

DD. Stephen's Creek Regt plus part of Dutch Fork Regt (Col. J. Cotton, Sr.)

EE. Fair Forest Regt plus part of Long Cane Regt (Col. D. Plummer)

FF. Spartan Regt plus part of Long Cane Regt (Col. A. Mills)

Patriot forces

A. Overmountain men, Washington Co., VA (Col. W. Campbell)

B. Overmountain men, Washington Co., NC (Lt. Col. J. Sevier)

C. Overmountain men, Sullivan Co., NC (Col. I. Shelby)

D. Militia, Chester Co. and York Co., SC (Col. J.Williams)

E. Militia, Columbia Co. and Elbert Co., GA (Maj. W. Chandler)

F. Militia, Chester Co. and York Co., SC (Col. E. Lacey)

G. Militia, Wilkes Co., NC (Col. B. Cleveland)

H. Militia, Lincoln Co., NC (Lt. Col. F. Hambright & Maj. W. Chronicle)

I. Militia, Surrey Co., NC (Maj. J. Winston)

J. Militia, Burke Co., NC (Maj. J. McDowell)

N

0   300yd
0   300m

Patriot forces

A. Overmountain men, Washington Co., VA (Col. W. Campbell)

B. Overmountain men, Washington Co., NC (Lt. Col. J. Sevier)

C. Overmountain men, Sullivan Co., NC (Col. I. Shelby)

D. Militia, Chester Co. and York Co., SC (Col. J.Williams)

E. Militia, Columbia Co. and Elbert Co., GA (Maj. W. Candler)

F. Militia, Chester Co. and York Co., SC (Col. E. Lacey)

G. Militia, Wilkes Co., NC (Col. B. Cleveland)

H. Militia, Lincoln Co., NC (Lt. Col. F. Hambright & Maj. W. Chronicle)

I. Militia, Surrey Co., NC (Maj. J. Winston)

J. Militia, Burke Co., NC (Maj. J. McDowell)

Loyalist forces

AA. Maj. P. Ferguson

BB. Detachments from the King's American Regt, New Jersey Volunteers, Loyal American Regt, and Royal American Volunteers (Capt. A. DePeyster & Capt. S. Ryerson)

○   Remnants of Loyalist militias

N

0   200yd
0   200m

INTO COMBAT

The ensuing battle played out organically, for the Patriots had no centralized command structure. Their march had ended about a half-mile from the southwestern end of Kings Mountain. The officers remained mounted; otherwise, horses were tied off, and personal gear stowed. Many of the men put aside their hats, tying handkerchiefs around their heads, which were less likely to become entangled in the forest fighting to come. Whatever their headgear, the militia then split into two columns in order to envelop the entire hill, each unit of men occupying positions at the base of the slope on both its northern and southern flanks.

On the southern flank, Campbell's 200 Virginians held the left of the line at the base of the hill, Major Joseph McDowell with 90 men the center, and Major Joseph Winston with 60 men the right. On the northern flank, Sevier's 120 men were stationed at the base of the hill. To his left, Shelby commanded 120 men; then Colonel James Williams with 30; Major William Candler with 30; Colonel Edward Lacey with 100; Cleveland with 110; and at the far end of the line, 50 men under Lieutenant Colonel Frederick Hambright. Winston and Hambright had the farthest to go to get into position, and were about ten minutes short of their jumping-off points when the fighting began.

"There was very little military subordination," Colonel William Hill noted, "as all that was required or expected was that every Officer & man should ascend the mountain so as to surround the enemy on all quarters which was promptly executed" (quoted in Salley 1921 :22–23). Teenaged Patriot Thomas Young recalled that the only orders he received were to raise a whoop when the first shot was fired, rush forward, and fight as best he could (Buchanan 2019: 230). Around 1400hrs, the Patriots began moving out, every man keeping four or five shots in his mouth, both to prevent thirst and aid a quick reload.

Ferguson, meanwhile, was still blissfully unaware his pickets had been silently eliminated and his position surrounded. The Loyalists were only alerted to the enemy's presence around 1500hrs when a single Patriot, understandably on edge, loosed a shot at what he thought was movement through the trees. Ferguson's camp immediately scrambled into action. Ferguson had the advantage of greater numbers – roughly 1,000 men to the Patriots' 910 – but of these, only approximately 100 were uniformed veterans of Crown service. Collectively dubbed the Provincials, they included detachments from the King's American Regiment, New Jersey Volunteers, Loyal American Regiment, and Prince of Wales' Royal American Volunteers. The Loyalists

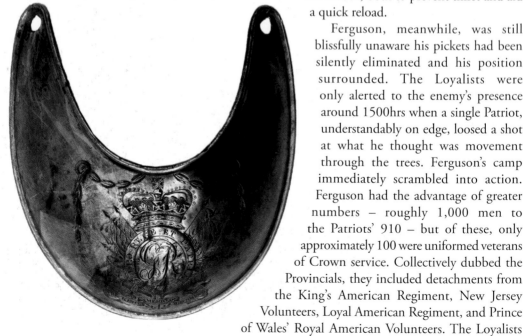

This gorget was worn by an officer of the King's American Regiment, which was raised on Staten Island, New York in 1776 by Edmund Fanning, who served as its colonel. Major actions in which the unit participated included the attacks on Fort Clinton and Fort Montgomery on the Hudson River in New York (1777), the defense of Newport, Rhode Island (1778), and the battle of Hobkirk's Hill in South Carolina (1781). (metmuseum.org/CC0 1.0)

recruited locally wore homespun frontier clothing no different from that of their Patriot neighbors on the other side. Ferguson had done his best to drill them, even resorting to the expedient of having issued them knives with their handles whittled down to the extent that each man could insert it in the barrel of his musket as a makeshift bayonet.

Though they had no targets, the Loyalists opened fire while the Patriots were still closing the net around them. It was Campbell who gave the signal to attack. "Here they are, my brave boys," he bellowed; "Shout like hell, and fight like devils!" (quoted in Draper 1881: 586). The woods immediately resounded with the howls and whoops of the line, spreading from unit to unit until the tumult rang in a complete circle around Kings Mountain. The psychological impact was as heartening to the Patriots as it was dispiriting to the Loyalists.

The steep flanks of the hill were heavily wooded, offering good cover but somewhat heavy going for an attacking force. The ascent in Campbell's sector was particularly rough and craggy. Ferguson ordered his Provincials to lead a bayonet charge that drove Campbell's men back down the south side of the slope, Lieutenant Anthony Allaire, mounted on a horse, cutting down a Patriot officer fleeing on foot with one blow of his sword. However, Shelby's men then commenced their assault on the opposite flank, forcing Ferguson to withdraw the Provincials, re-form them at the summit, and send them charging down the hill's north face.

Leading from the front, Patriot officers were prominent targets. Captain Moses Shelby was wounded twice and forced to retire from the action. Lacey led his men forward and immediately had his horse shot from under him, as

Having tied off their horses, the Patriots begin the ascent up the slopes of Kings Mountain. At least five African Americans participated in the Patriot assault, including Essius/ Esaius Bowman, who served in Captain Joel Lewis' company from Virginia and is said to have been one of the men who shot Major Patrick Ferguson; Ishmael Titus, a slave from Rowan County, North Carolina, who substituted for his master's draft call-up in exchange for his freedom and served in Captain John Cleveland's company; Andrew Ferguson, who also saw action at Musgrove Mill, Cowpens, Guilford Courthouse, Ninety Six, and Eutaw Springs; and Primes/Primus, another veteran of the battles at Camden, Cowpens, Guilford Courthouse, Eutaw Springs, and the siege of Yorktown. (Interim Archives/ Getty Images)

Kings Mountain, October 7, 1780

Patriot view: Patriot militiamen at the forested base of Kings Mountain can glimpse the bare crest of the slope running horizontally roughly southwest to northeast. Scattered throughout the higher ground in the distance are the Loyalist enemy, crouched behind boulders or trees, firing downhill toward their Patriot adversaries. Some of these marksmen are so well concealed only the puffs of smoke from their shots give away their positions. Those Loyalists who can be seen are local recruits, not in uniform. The more immediate threat is presented by the uniformed Loyalists charging downhill in a bid to break the Patriot cordon closing up around Kings Mountain. Veterans from a number of Provincial units were present at the battle; in this sector, bayonets presented, are troops of the King's American Regiment, their muskets fitted with the 17in-long bayonets the Patriots had come to respect and fear at close quarters. This is not their first assault; after repeatedly charging downhill and then clambering back up again to regroup they are sweaty and exhausted. Scattered across the slope are the bodies of the dead and dying left behind from their previous charges.

Loyalist view: As the Loyalists charge downhill they once again see their elusive enemy start to turn and run before their frustrated foe can get to grips with them. For every Patriot in view there are many more taking cover behind trees, either firing or reloading. There is no uniformity in the Patriot ranks, which are comprised of militia from the surrounding counties and the tall, raw-boned Overmountain men from the far side of the Allegheny Mountains. They are armed with the usual miscellany of muskets and Pennsylvania or Kentucky Long Rifles, with every man bearing his own personal powder horn, shot pouch, canteen, and *mêlée* weapon (such as a hatchet or knife). The only insignia is a white rag or piece of paper tucked somewhere in each volunteer's hat or the handkerchief tied around his head. Patriot officers are outfitted no differently from the men under their command, but while the rank and file have tied off their horses well to the rear, their officers remain mounted. Leading from the front in this conspicuous role, casualties among the officers are high, but the pressure they maintain upon the bodies of the enemy is inexorable and ultimately proves to be decisive.

did Cleveland. Captain William Edmondson and Lieutenant Reece Bowen of Campbell's regiment both fell fighting.

So far, the action had been concentrated at the western end of Kings Mountain. As Campbell described it, "Col. Shelby's regiment and mine began the attack, and sustained the whole fire of the enemy for about ten minutes, while the other troops were forming around the height" (quoted in Draper 1881: 526). The last Patriot units finally closed the circle at the eastern end of the line when Winston and Hambright took up station, cutting off Ferguson's last chance to escape. Raising his hat over his head as a rallying point, 25-year-old Major William Chronicle, at the head of Hambright's men, was immediately shot dead, but the Patriots nevertheless doggedly set off up the slope. Ferguson responded by ordering his Provincials to this threatened sector; they unleashed a volley, which killed Captain John Mattocks, then launched into another bayonet charge. Despite being wounded twice, Captain William Lenoir rallied the faltering militia.

Cleveland's regiment began its advance up the hill. Again, casualties were particularly severe among the officers. Captain Minor Smith, Lieutenant Samuel Johnson, and no fewer than three members of the same family – the brothers Major Micajah Lewis, Captain Joel Lewis, and Lieutenant James M. Lewis – were all wounded. Even as these men fell, however, increasing numbers of Patriots were fighting their way ever closer to the Loyalists clustered along the skyline. Meanwhile, the seesaw struggle at the western end of the line continued. A pattern had swiftly emerged, whereby the Loyalists would charge and drive the Patriots downhill at bayonet point, only for the Patriots to regroup, countercharge, and shoot down the Loyalists as they clambered back up the hill to its summit. The Patriot officers were aware their men could not resist "cold steel," and did not oblige them to; their role was to rally and re-form their ranks after each charge, to ensure retreat did not become rout.

The crux of the battle arrived when, according to Loyalist Captain Abraham dePeyster, his King's American Regiment charged the Patriots and drove the right wing of them back down the hill in confusion. This was in Shelby's sector. As he described it:

> In the course of the battle we were repeatedly repulsed by the enemy and driven down the mountain. In this succession of repulses and attacks, and in giving succour [sic] to the points hardest pressed, much disorder took place in our ranks: the men of my column, of Campbell's column and a great part of Sevier's, were mingled together in the confusion of the battle. Toward the latter part of the action, the enemy made a fierce and gallant charge upon us from the summit of the mountain, and drove us near to the foot of it. The retreat was so rapid that there was great danger of its becoming a rout. (Quoted in Draper 1881: 565)

The wavering Patriots might have broken but, according to dePeyster, Ferguson signaled with his silver whistle for the Provincials to withdraw, being afraid the enemy would get possession of the height from the other flank. The Loyalist militia, observing the retreat and being ignorant of the cause, panicked. Taking advantage of the enemy's sudden disarray, Shelby, Campbell, and Sevier were able to rally their men and lead them on a final

Like many American firearms of the Colonial era, this rifle is fitted with an imported barrel and lock, which comes from a French Modèle 1728 infantry musket, and bears the marking of the royal arms factory at Saint-Étienne. (metmuseum.org/CC0 1.0)

This dragoon saber, manufactured by Loyalist James Potter in New York City, features a brass and iron mounted hilt fitted to a 25in-long, slightly curved, single-edged, plain blade with a rounded point. The one-piece grip is crafted from wood carved in a spiral pattern, with a brass hilt and brass base attached. The style was commonly used by cavalry on both sides throughout the war. (Photo © Don Troiani/Bridgeman Images)

charge that this time reached the summit of Kings Mountain. With the Loyalist militias fleeing east along the ridgeline, the depleted Provincials were forced to withdraw with them.

There was still fight left in the Loyalists – Hambright, with three fresh bullet holes through his hat, was shot through his thigh, a severed artery swiftly filling his boot with blood. As the Loyalist position at the western end of the line collapsed, however, the Patriots began to close in from all sides. Sensing the inevitable, some Loyalists began on their own initiative to display flags of surrender. Ferguson rode up and cut them down with his sword; but his position was becoming hopeless. Finally, out of options, he determined to break out, accompanied by two officers, Colonel Vezey Husband and Major Daniel Plummer. All three men mounted up and rode hard for the east in a desperate bid to reach Cornwallis and safety – but the Patriots had been counting on just such an eventuality. It was well known that Ferguson, who had already had two horses shot out from under him, wielded his sword in his left hand, and that he wore a conspicuously light-checked hunting shirt. Patriot marksmen now easily picked him out, and long before he had cleared their lines they riddled his body with bullets. Lifeless, he tumbled backward, but with one foot still wedged in the stirrup he was dragged along the ground some distance by his heedless horse. Husband and Plummer, too, were both shot out of their saddles, the former fatally, the latter so badly wounded he was left for dead, though he ultimately recovered.

The Patriots pushing east along the ridge, meanwhile, drove the Loyalists back toward their encampment, where they made a last stand. Patriot John Craig later described how "we succeeded in gaining the top of the mountain and driving them before us … to where they had formed something like a hollow square out of their wagons. This at any rate presented the appearance of a temporary breastwork" (quoted in Dunkerly 2007: 39). Some 20 mounted Provincials charged the oncoming Patriots but were rapidly picked-off by sharpshooting riflemen. Even now, there was still some kick in the resistance. Shelby, leading from the front, narrowly cheated death when a Loyalist musket discharged directly alongside the left side of his face; while the hair on the left side of his head was scorched off, the ball flew harmlessly away.

With the Loyalists hemmed into an increasingly tight space, assailed on all sides, and their unit cohesion having totally collapsed, the battle was degenerating into a slaughter. White flags again began to appear in the Loyalist lines, but at first to no effect – the first two men to raise these tokens of surrender were gunned down. Even after the capitulation was recognized, "we killed near a hundred of them," Lieutenant Joseph Hughes later shrugged, "and could hardly be restrained from killing the whole of them" (quoted in Draper 1881: 285).

The entire Loyalist force trapped on Kings Mountain when the battle commenced had, in the space of an hour, ceased to exist. Shelby calculated the loss incurred by Ferguson's Provincials at 30 killed, 28 wounded, and 57 prisoners. The Loyalist militias lost 127 killed, 125 wounded, and 649 prisoners, bringing the total casualty count to 157 killed, 153 wounded, and 706 prisoners, or 1,016 in all. The Loyalist dead were interred without ceremony in a mass grave. The Patriots reported 28 killed and 62 wounded,

disproportionately officers, striking proof of the role they were expected to play in leading their men from the front.

The Patriots did not linger to savor their triumph. The Overmountain men were aware that by marching east they had left their homesteads denuded of manpower and open to raids by those First Nations allied to the British. In addition, no-one wanted to risk incurring Tarleton's wrath by loitering too long in open country. The Patriot force split up as its constituent militias drifted away to their home counties.

The cost to those communities on both sides sundered by the war would be heavy. Four brothers from Lincoln County, North Carolina, served at Kings Mountain – William and Joseph Logan, with the Patriots, and John and Thomas Logan, with the Loyalists. At least four brothers from the Goforth family, of Rutherford County, North Carolina, also participated in the battle, Preston, Jr. with the Patriots, the other three with the Loyalists. All four were killed.

What explains the outcome at Kings Mountain? Responsibility for the Loyalist debacle must ultimately lie entirely with Ferguson. Even after stirring up the hornets' nest among the Overmountain men he still had plenty of time to fall back to Charlotte with his fresh recruits. He knew he was being pursued, but his response was fatally compromised; he was too slow both in the pace of his retreat and in requesting reinforcements from Cornwallis; and in the end, the location where he elected to stand his ground doomed him and the men under his command, for in reality, the heights of Kings Mountain afforded only the illusion of security. The reasons for this were outlined in detail by Loyalist Captain Alexander Chesney:

The death of Major Patrick Ferguson, whose desperate bid to escape the trap into which he had led his company stood no chance of success. To Patriot militiaman James Collins, who inspected Ferguson's corpse, "it appeared that almost fifty rifles must have been leveled at him, at the same time; seven rifle balls had passed through his body, both of his arms were broken, and his hat and clothing was literally shot to pieces" (Collins 1859: 54). Although his tactical leadership was fatally flawed, the loss of Ferguson was a serious one for the Royalist cause, as he was one of the few regular British officers who could inspire the confidence of Loyalist American volunteers. (Library of Congress)

A rare personal clash played out during the battle of Cowpens on January 17, 1781, Brigadier General Daniel Morgan's brilliant set-piece victory over British forces under Lieutenant-Colonel Banastre Tarleton. As Tarleton fled in the aftermath he was overtaken by Lieutenant Colonel William Washington, and hand-to-hand fighting broke out between the two men and their entourages. Washington was about to be cut down by Thomas Patterson, a cornet of the 17th Light Dragoons, when Patterson was shot by Washington's orderly trumpeter, as depicted in this 1845 painting by the American artist William Ranney (1813–57). The orderly's surname has never been verified; it was possibly Ball, Collin, or Collins. It is known that seven African Americans served in the Patriot ranks at Cowpens, four of them freemen. (MPI/Getty Images)

Kings Mountain from its height would have enabled us to oppose a superior force with advantage, had it not been covered with wood which sheltered the Americans and enabled them to fight in their favorite manner; in fact after driving in our piquets they were able to advance in three divisions under separate leaders to the crest of the hill in perfect safety until they took post and opened an irregular but destructive fire from behind trees and other cover … in this manner the engagement was maintained near an hour, the mountaineers flying whenever there was danger of being charged by the Bayonet and returning again so soon as the British detachment had faced about to repel another of their parties. (Quoted in Ferguson 1888: 107)

While the Patriots were firing uphill at targets silhouetted against the clear blue sky, the Loyalists were firing downhill at elusive figures flitting through the trees. As he came under fire, the teenage James Collins immediately appreciated the difference: "The shot of the enemy soon began to pass over us like hail" (Collins 1859: 52). The Loyalists had seized the high ground, but in the end, Collins concluded, "Their great elevation above us had proved their ruin; they overshot us altogether, scarce touching a man, except those on horseback, while every rifle from below, seemed to have the desired effect" (Collins 1859: 53).

The significance of the outcome at Kings Mountain was appreciated on both sides at the highest level. Lieutenant-General Sir Henry Clinton considered it the first link in a chain of events that culminated in the British loss of America, a perspective endorsed by Thomas Jefferson who, reminiscing more than four decades later, called it "the joyful annunciation of that turn of the tide of success which terminated the Revolutionary War, with the seal of our independence" (Founders Online).

Analysis

When he arrived in Cambridge, Massachusetts, on July 2, 1775, to take command of the war effort in New England, George Washington was distinctly unimpressed with the local militia at his disposal. They were of an "exceedingly dirty and nasty" disposition, in his estimation; their vices reflected "an unaccountable kind of stupidity in the lower classes of these people" (Founders Online). Yet it was precisely these dirty, nasty, stupid, lower-class people who had nearly overwhelmed British Regulars during their retreat from Concord on April 19, given them a bloody nose at Bunker Hill on June 17, and kept them confined to Boston subsequently, in a siege that culminated with the evacuation of Crown forces on March 17, 1776.

Washington never warmed to the potential, or appreciated the contribution of, such men. "'Tis time we should get rid of an error which the experience of all mankind has exploded, and which our own experience has dearly taught us to reject," he explained in a circular to the state governments on October 18, 1780, namely,

> the carrying on a War with militia, or, which is nearly the same thing, temporary levies against a regular permanent and disciplined force. The Idea is chimerical, and that we have so long persisted in it, is a reflection on the judgment of a nation so enlightened as we are, as well as a strong proof of the empire of prejudice over Reason. If we continue in the infatuation, we shall deserve to lose the object we are contending for. (Founders Online)

Washington yearned to fight a conventional war of maneuver with a professional army, to win the decisive victory, to emulate Hannibal, Pyrrhus, and Caesar; but he was not the man for this task. His gifts of command were prodigious – his iron will was the only force capable of keeping the Continental Army in the field during the dark days of its misfortune, through the relentless winters of defeat and deprivation, and in line once it had triumphed, when the rank and file were ready to march on Philadelphia. Nevertheless, whenever presented with the opportunity to exhibit tactical genius on the battlefield, such qualities eluded him. His record in set-piece confrontations with the British – at Brooklyn, White Plains, Brandywine, Germantown, Monmouth – was a poor one. Even his pivotal triumph at Yorktown was owed to the presence of a French expeditionary force and the French navy.

Had Washington ever been able to command the Continental Army on a European scale he craved and stake the future of the Revolution on a single clash of arms, the ensuing defeat may well have been disastrous, either because the Patriot cause simply expired on that day or, even if it did ultimately succeed, because the fledgling republic would not have had the deified Washington we recognize to guide it through the tempestuous early years of its existence. It is a supreme irony that Washington's sole martial masterpiece, his critical moonlit victory at Trenton, reflected the tactical approach of the militia commanders he never truly understood – attacking under cover of darkness and rough weather, employing local knowledge, improvisation, surprise, and a swift withdrawal in the face of superior opposition. It was these methods that slowly bled the British and cost them hearts and minds wherever they might temporarily triumph. In the final analysis, it was Washington who held the line before the British advance, but it was the militias who won over the country behind the Redcoats' backs.

The British were entirely aware they lacked the manpower to effectively suppress the entirety of so vast an expanse as the colonies. Only with local support could they hope to accomplish this, and the wishful thinking that such support existed motivated much of the Crown's strategic goal setting over the course of the war. British assumptions that loyalism represented the silent majority throughout their erstwhile colonies proved chimerical, however, and the fitful progress of the Royal war effort repeatedly contributed to tragic episodes of miscommunication even in those specific locales where Loyalist sentiment did prevail, whereby the Loyalists would rise in anticipation of linking up with the British only to be crushed by the more responsive Patriots before Crown forces could arrive. Even where British policy was relatively successful – in the exploitation of existing partnerships with the First Nations and the extemporized recruitment of fugitive slaves – the backlash to such policies amid a colonial population that largely defined itself in opposition to

This memorial in Van Cortlandt Park in the Bronx, New York, is located in what is now called Indian Field, in honor of the Stockbridge First Nations warriors who perished there in the Patriot cause on August 31, 1778, including their *sachem* (chief), Daniel Nimham, and his son Abraham. This victory nearly ended the career of Lieutenant-Colonel Banastre Tarleton before he gained notoriety for his actions; unhorsed in the charge, a Stockbridge warrior would have finished him off after he hit the ground, but had already discharged his musket, which lacked a bayonet. (Author)

precisely those two constituencies probably succeeded only in driving more fence sitters into the Patriot camp than were gained.

Unsurprisingly, given they derived from the same background, Loyalist volunteers were man for man a match for their Patriot equivalents. Patrick Ferguson was impressed with the caliber of the men he recruited in the Carolinas, whose backcountry ruggedness rendered them a good fit for irregular warfare, being consistently excellent woodsmen and marksmen.

It was qualities of leadership that made the intangible yet decisive difference. It was men such as Francis Marion, Isaac Shelby, Andrew Pickens, and Elijah Clarke who established the critical edge maintained by the Patriot militias over their Loyalist counterparts. The hidebound nature of British military tradition contributed to this. Regardless of demonstrated ability, the British refused to extend anything like

equal status to Loyalist officers. Lesser discriminations (such as the refusal to grant half-pay pensions) and the failure to supply and equip Loyalist units on equal terms with the Regulars discouraged many who would have been eager to fight for their country via service to their king. In the final analysis, at the grassroots level, the men who accepted leadership roles on the Patriot side commanded greater respect in their communities; and the rank and file under their command were derived from those communities, whereas the Loyalists were at best exiles and as often as not unwelcome outsiders. Aware of this alienation, the Loyalists drifted ever closer to dependence on the British, which only further weakened both their ability to act independently and their claim to be fighting for a national cause and not on behalf of an occupying imperial power. Ironically, when its own turn came to raise indigenous militias to help relieve the burden on its regular troops and ultimately emerge as a national army, from Vietnam to Afghanistan, the United States would find itself trapped in the same dilemma.

In many ways, therefore, the Loyalists were as much a burden to the Crown as they were an asset, and a sense of profound disappointment pervades the correspondence of prominent British policy and war makers regarding them. "I have too often observed, that when the Storm appears, our friends disappear," Cornwallis concluded; however, he also conceded "The patience with which they endure the most cruel torments and suffer the most violent oppressions that a country ever labored under, convince me that they are sincere, at least as far as their affection to the cause of Great Britain" (quoted in Stevens 1888: 264).

This memorial commemorates one of the worst disasters suffered by Patriot forces in Westchester County. It is sited at the location of Joseph Young's house, a Patriot headquarters that was raided on December 24, 1778, by Loyalists under Major Mansfield Bearmore, 40 Patriots, including Young, being taken prisoner. Subsequently reoccupied by the Patriots, on February 3, 1780, Young's House was garrisoned by 250 Continentals led by Lieutenant Colonel Joseph Thompson. Early that morning, a mixed force of British regulars, Hessians, and a company of mounted Loyalists led by James DeLancey overwhelmed the garrison, burnt Young's House to the ground with several wounded Continentals trapped inside, and took 76 prisoners, including Thompson. (Author)

Aftermath

OPPOSITE

Titled "Tory Refugees on the Way to Canada," this illustration by Howard Pyle (1853-1911) was published in 1901. Under the terms of the Treaty of Paris, which ended the American Revolutionary War on September 3, 1783, the United State Congress pledged it would recommend its constituent members "provide for the restitution of all estates, rights, and properties" forfeited by the Loyalists over the past eight years. In reality, many Loyalists found themselves frozen out from their prewar assets and unwelcome in their old communities. Many spent years seeking compensation from the Crown, and at least 75,000 departed for other shores in a global diaspora. (Public Domain)

Kings Mountain was a critical turning point, but the war raged on throughout the South. Patriot irregulars were seconded to the new Continental Army led by Major General Nathanael Greene, who understood their limitations and used them to his advantage. They served the cause to best effect in the guerrilla war that played out in South Carolina on a parallel track to the formal fencing between Greene and Cornwallis.

Although he gained his revenge on Tarleton on November 20, 1780, the impetuous dragoon leader suffering his first defeat when the militia bloodily repulsed him at Blackstock's Farm, Sumter was defeated by South Carolina Loyalists under Fraser at Lynches Creek on March 6, 1781. Nevertheless, with Cornwallis having taken the fighting core of the Crown's forces with him on his fateful march into Virginia, the momentum overall was clearly with the Patriots.

The British evacuated Camden on May 9. Sometimes working together, Lee and Marion forced the surrender of Fort Watson on April 23, Fort Motte on May 12, Fort Granby on May 15, and Fort Galphin on May 21. The Loyalists lost any hope of direct British support when the garrison at Georgetown evacuated on May 28. Lee then linked up with the Patriot forces under Elijah Clarke besieging Augusta, which was defended by Thomas Brown and a motley collection of his Rangers, local militia, and Cherokees, Creeks, and Chickasaws. Brown finally yielded Augusta on June 5.

The Loyalists at Ninety Six, meanwhile, endured an epic siege from May 21 to June 21 only for the settlement to be abandoned on July 8. Marion scored another victory with an ambush at Parker's Ferry on the Pon Pon River on August 30. By the end of the year, other than the Loyalist enclaves still under Crown authority at Charleston and Savannah, Georgia and the Carolinas were entirely in Patriot hands. Despite, or perhaps because of, their deteriorating strategic situation, the increasingly desperate Loyalists intensified the brutality of their resistance. The endemic nature of partisan warfare in the South poisoned the minds of its participants.

Captain William "Bloody Bill" Cunningham and his Loyalist militia, dubbed the "Bloody Scout," routinely murdered captured Patriots. Patriot leaders such as Colonel Benjamin "Bull Dog" Cleveland and Colonel Griffith Rutherford responded in kind. When a Patriot militia under Colonel Elijah Clarke defeated a Loyalist militia under Major James Dunlap at Beattie's Mill, South Carolina, on March 23, 1781, Dunlap was taken prisoner and subsequently murdered. Colonel Andrew Pickens, whose home Dunlap had torched the previous year, shrugged off the incident, for Loyalists under Colonel Hezekiah Williams had captured his brother, John, and turned him over to the Cherokees, who allegedly burned him to death.

Under the terms of the Treaty of Paris, which ended the American Revolutionary War on September 3, 1783, those who had fought for the Crown were entitled to remain in the fledgling United States of America. Many elected to do so, gradually fading into the social fabric of the new republic. Many others elected to depart, however, or were forced to do so through the ostracism or intimidation of their erstwhile neighbors. Some entire communities were uprooted; the return of Florida to Spain was a bitter blow to those refugees who had fled there and begun rebuilding their lives only to now press on again into an unknown future.

Worst afflicted were those left behind, those most desperately loyal to the Crown. While the white Loyalists could be evacuated and compensated, the First Nations peoples who had sided with the British were left friendless and alone on their ancestral lands. As always, the most vulnerable – America's enslaved – received the least consideration. The unresolved legacy of this inherent contradiction coded into the formation of the United States of America by those very Patriots who had fought for her independence – the persistence of slavery in a land of liberty – would only be resolved by another civil war less than 80 years later.

ABOVE RIGHT
Agrippa Hull, depicted here in later life, fought with the Patriots in the American Revolutionary War. Although the role played by African Americans in the Patriot cause was sometimes acknowledged, those who had found themselves on the Loyalist side received brutal treatment. During the war, runaway slaves had fled to such island refuges off the South Carolina and Georgia coast as Sullivan's, Tybee, Pace's, James, and Daufuskie. The British evacuated the fugitives who made it to their lines in time, but those left behind were abandoned to their own devices. As late as 1787 there were still hundreds of black Loyalist irregulars, veterans of Crown service, at large in a maroon colony hidden in the swamps of the Savannah River. The final suppression of this group in May 1787 represented the last shots of the American Revolutionary War. (Universal History Archive/Getty Images)

SELECT BIBLIOGRAPHY

Allen, Thomas B. (2010). *Tories: Fighting for the King in America's First Civil War*. New York, NY: HarperCollins.

Beach, Allen C. (1879) *The Centennial Celebrations of the State of New York*. Albany, NY: Weed, Parsons & Co.

Bell, J.L. (2020). "The Fighting Ground 'between the Enemy & the American force,'" *Boston 1775*, January 20, 2020, http://boston1775.blogspot.com/2020/01/the-fighting-ground-between-enemy.html

Bolton, Charles K. (1902). *Letters of Hugh Earl Percy*. Boston, MA: Charles E. Goodspeed.

Buchanan, John (2019). *The Road to Charleston: Nathanael Greene and the American Revolution*. Charlottesville, VA: University of Virginia Press.

Bunce, Oliver B. (1870). *The Romance of the Revolution*. Philadelphia, PA: Porter & Coates.

Callahan, North (1963). *Royal Raiders: The Tories of the American Revolution*. New York, NY: Bobbs-Merrill.

Campbell, William M. (1849). *The Border Warfare of New York During the Revolution*. New York, NY: Baker & Scribner.

Cashin, Edward J. (1999). *The King's Ranger: Thomas Brown and the American Revolution on the Southern Frontier*. New York, NY: Fordham University Press.

Clinton, George (1900). *Public Papers of George Clinton, First Governor of New York, 1777–1795, 1801–1804*, v. 3. Albany, NY: James B. Lyon.

Clinton, George (1901). *Public Papers of George Clinton, First Governor of New York, 1777–1795, 1801–1804*, v. 5. Albany, NY: James B. Lyon.

Clinton, George (1902). *Public Papers of George Clinton, First Governor of New York, 1777–1795, 1801–1804*, v. 6. Albany, NY: James B. Lyon.

Collins, James P. (1859). *A Revolutionary Soldier*. Clinton, LA: Feliciana Democrat.

Cutter, William (1861). *The Life of Israel Putnam, Major-General in the Army of the American Revolution*. New York, NY: Derby & Jackson.

Draper, Lyman C. (1881). *King's Mountain and Its Heroes*. Cincinnati, OH: P.G. Thomson.

Dunkerly, Robert M. (2007). *The Battle of Kings Mountain: Eyewitness Accounts*. Charleston, SC: The History Press.

Dwight, Timothy (1822). *Travels in New-England and New-York, Vol. III*. New Haven, CT: S. Converse.

Ferguson, James (1888). *Two Scottish Soldiers*. Aberdeen: D. Wyllie & Son.

Graham, W.A. (1904). *General Joseph Graham and his Papers on North Carolina Revolutionary History*. Raleigh, NC: Edwards & Broughton.

Gray, Robert (1910). "Colonel Robert Gray's Observations on the War in Carolina," *The South Carolina Historical and Genealogical Magazine* 11.3: 139–59.

Hanger, George (1789). *An Address to the Army; in reply to Strictures, by Roderick M'Kenzie (late Lieutenant in the 71st Regiment) on Tarleton's History of the Campaigns of 1780 and 1781*. London: James Ridgway.

Heath, William (1901). *Memoirs of Major-General William Heath*. New York, NY: William Abbatt.

Hufeland, Otto (1982). *Westchester County during the American Revolution, 1775–1783*. Harrison, NY: Harbor Hill Books.

Kwasny, Mark V. (1996). *Washington's Partisan War, 1775–1783*. Kent, OH: Kent State University Press.

Lee, Henry (1827). Memoirs of the War in the Southern Department of the United States. Washington, DC.: Peter Force.

Moore, Frank (1876). *The Diary of the Revolution*. Hartford, CT: J.B. Burr.

Moore, George H. (1908). "Historical Notes on the Employment of Negroes in the American Army of the Revolution," *Magazine of History* 1.1-4: 13–68.

National Park Service (no date). *Teaching with Historic Places: The Battle of Oriskany*. https://www.nps.gov/teachers/classrooms/upload/TwHP-Lessons_79oriskany.pdf

National Park Service (2009). *Oriskany: A Place of Great Sadness*. http://npshistory.com/publications/fost/ser.pdf

Paine, Thomas (1817). *The Political Works of Thomas Paine*. London: W.T. Sherwin.

Piecuch, Jim (2013). *Three Peoples, One King: Loyalists, Indians, and Slaves in the Revolutionary South, 1775–1782*. Columbia, SC: University of South Carolina Press.

Proceedings of the Massachusetts Historical Society 6, 1863. Boston, MA.

Salley, Jr., A.S., ed. (1921). *Colonel William Hill's Memoirs of the Revolution*. Columbia, SC: Lillie.

Sargent, Winthrop (1861). *The Life and Career of Major John André*. Boston, MA: Ticknor & Fields.

Simcoe, John G. (1844). *Simcoe's Military Journal*. New York, NY: Bartlett & Welford.

Simms, William G. (1846). *The Life of Francis Marion*. New York, NY: G.F. Cooledge & Brother.

Stevens, Benjamin F. (1888). *The Campaign in Virginia, 1781. An exact Reprint of Six rare Pamphlets on the Clinton-Cornwallis Controversy*. London: privately published.

Stevens, Paul L. (1984). "His Majesty's 'Savage' Allies: British Policy and the Northern Indians during the Revolutionary War: The Carleton Years, 1774–1778." PhD dissertation, State University of New York at Buffalo.

Stone, William L. (1851). *Life of Joseph Brant*. Buffalo, NY: Phinney & Co.

Tarleton, Banastre (1787). *A History of Campaigns of 1780 and 1781 in the Southern Provinces of North America*. Dublin: Colles, Exshaw, et al.

Thacher, James (1827). *A Military Journal during the American Revolutionary War, from 1775 to 1783*. Boston, MA: John Cotton.

Tiedemann, Joseph S., Eugene R. Fingerhut & Robert W. Venables, eds (2010). *The Other Loyalists: Ordinary People, Royalism, and the Revolution in the Middle Colonies, 1763–1787*. Albany, NY: State University of New York Press.

Ward, Harry M. (2002). *Between the Lines: Banditti of the American Revolution*. Westport, CT: Praeger.

Watt, Gavin K. (1997). *The Burning of the Valleys: Daring Raids from Canada against the New York Frontier in the Fall of 1780*. Toronto: Dundurn.

Watt, Gavin K. (2011). *Rebellion in the Mohawk Valley: The St. Leger Expedition of 1777*. Toronto: Dundurn.

Willett, William M. (1831). *A Narrative of the Military Actions of Colonel Marinus Willett*. New York, NY: G. & C. & H. Carvill.

Websites

Journal of the American Revolution, https://allthingsliberty.com/

The King's Men: Loyalist Military Units, http://www.nyhistory.net/drums/kingsmen.htm

The Online Institute for Advanced Loyalist Studies, http://www.royalprovincial.com/index.htm

"Founders Online," The US National Archives, https://founders.archives.gov/

The memorial in the foreground, located in the First Presbyterian Church Cemetery on Crompond Road, Yorktown, in Westchester County, New York, marks the gravesite of Colonel Christopher Greene and Major Ebenezer Flagg of the 1st Rhode Island Regiment, Continental Army, who were killed during the Loyalist raid on Pines Bridge, May 14, 1781. The original church on this site was erected in 1738. It served as a storehouse for the Continental Army during the Revolutionary War, and was burned to the ground by the British in 1779. The current church dates from 1799. (Author)

INDEX

References to illustrations are shown in **bold**.
References to plates are shown in bold with
caption pages in brackets, e.g. **48–49**, (50).